Shakespeare's Repentance Plays

Shakespeare's Repentance Plays:

The Search for an Adequate Form

ALAN R. VELIE

Rutherford • Madison • Teaneck
Fairleigh Dickinson University Press

© 1972 by Associated University Presses, Inc.

Associated University Presses, Inc.
Cranbury, New Jersey 08512

Library of Congress Cataloging in Publication Data

Velie, Alan R   1937–
  Shakespeare's repentance plays.

  Bibliography: p.
  1. Shakespeare, William, 1564–1616—Knowledge—
Repentance. 1. Title.
PR3069.R4V4   822.3′3   72-422
ISBN 0-8386-1126-5

Printed in the United States of America

To my wife

Contents

Contents

Acknowledgment

I am especially grateful to Professor Virgil K. Whitaker of Stanford University who, from my first graduate seminar in Shakespeare to the last draft of the dissertation that became this book, was of inestimable help. I also owe a considerable debt to my parents for helping to pull the book into shape, and to my wife for her help at all stages of the project.

Introduction

The doctrine of repentance was a matter of utmost importance to Elizabethans. According to E. M. W. Tillyard, "the theological scheme of sin and salvation" was to Elizabethans the most essential part of Christian doctrine. Tillyard reminds us that

> the part of Christianity that was paramount (in Elizabethan times) was not the life of Christ but the orthodox scheme of the revolt of the bad angels, the creation, the temptation and the fall of man, the incarnation, the atonement, and regeneration through Christ . . . we should never let ourselves forget that the orthodox scheme of salvation was pervasive in the Elizabethan age.[1]

In a time in which virtually everyone believed literally in the rewards of heaven and the terrors of hell, the achievement of salvation was one of man's most important concerns. And the only way for sinful man to achieve salvation was through repentance. Elizabethans heard this doctrine constantly. One of their primary sources of religious instruction was the Homilies, which were read in all English churches every Sunday. Since church attendance was compulsory, over a period of years the ideas of the Homilies were hammered home.[2]

The Homily "Of Repentance" minces no words on the importance of repentance. It begins:

---

1. *The Elizabethan World Picture* (New York, 1944), p. 19.
2. Alfred Hart, *Shakespeare and the Homilies* (Melbourne, 1934), pp. 17–76.

There is nothing that the Holy Ghost doth so much labour in all the Scriptures to beat into men's heads, as Repentance, amendment of life, and speedy returning unto the Lord God of hosts. And no marvel why; for we do daily and hourly fall away from God, thereby purchasing unto ourselves, if he should deal with us according to his justice, eternal damnation.[3]

Since it was the principal means of thwarting eternal damnation, repentance was of major concern to the Elizabethans.

Like his contemporaries, Shakespeare was vitally interested in the doctrine of repentance. He returns to it time and again throughout his career. *The Two Gentlemen of Verona, Much Ado about Nothing, All's Well That Ends Well, Measure for Measure, Cymbeline, The Winter's Tale,* and *The Tempest* all make use of the doctrine in one way or another. The purpose of this book is to show that an important key to understanding these plays lies in recognizing that they deal with sin and repentance. Furthermore, it is to show how the plays deal with the doctrine. In *Two Gentlemen, Much Ado,* and *All's Well,* Shakespeare uses repentance as a plot device. In *Measure for Measure, Cymbeline,* and *The Winter's Tale,* he makes a serious study of the mental processes of a man who sins and repents. In *The Tempest* he looks at sin and repentance from the standpoint of the victim.

In exploring Shakespeare's use of the doctrine of repentance, I have found, moreover, that the traditional categories in which critics commonly group Shakespeare's plays are inaccurate. Those familiar with these categories will recognize *Two Gentlemen* and *Much Ado* as "romantic comedies," *All's Well* and *Measure for Measure* as

---

3. *Certain Sermons or Homilies Appointed to be Read in Churches in the Time of Queen Elizabeth of Famous Memory* (Oxford, 1844), p. 525.

"problem plays," and *Cymbeline, The Winter's Tale,* and
The Tempest as "romances." In important respects, however, *All's Well* should not be grouped with *Measure for
Measure,* but with *Two Gentlemen* and *Much Ado. All's
Well, Two Gentlemen,* and *Much Ado* emphasize highly
artificial intrigue plots, and deal with sin and repentance
superficially. *Measure for Measure,* on the other hand, is
a far more serious play. It resembles Shakespeare's tragedies of the same period in that the protagonist's moral
choices provide the mainspring of the action. In the tragedies the hero chooses to sin, and ruin follows. In *Measure
for Measure* the protagonist sins and falls, but his repentance brings redemption.

In *Measure for Measure* the plot devices of low comedy—the head trick and the bed trick—compromise the
serious theme. In his next repentance plays, Shakespeare
abandons comedy as a vehicle for the sin-repentance theme,
and experiments with melodrama. *Cymbeline* and *The Winter's Tale* are sophisticated variations of a crude form of
melodrama popular in Shakespeare's day. Melodrama,
which combines the happy ending of comedy with the serious tone and action of tragedy, proves a suitable vehicle
for a serious treatment of sin and repentance. In *The
Tempest* Shakespeare returns to comedy. Critics traditionally group *The Tempest* with *Cymbeline* and *The Winter's
Tale,* but in plot structure, if not in tone and seriousness of
theme, it is actually closer to *Much Ado about Nothing.*

Since they merely use repentance as a plot device, I shall
treat *Two Gentlemen, Much Ado* and *All's Well* cursorily
and will devote considerably more attention to the plays
that examine repentance seriously: *Measure for Measure,
Cymbeline,* and *The Winter's Tale.* Although other critics
have referred to Aquinas, Luther, and "the early divines"

as authorities,[4] I shall use the Homily "Of Repentance" as my sole authority for Elizabethan ideas about repentance. Just how Shakespeare is supposed to have been familiar with Aquinas and Luther is not clear. The only document that we can be sure he knew is the Homily, which, as was mentioned before, was read regularly in all English churches throughout his lifetime. His use of other homilies is well documented.[5]

Catholic and Protestant ideas on repentance varied somewhat. For instance, the Homily puts more emphasis on faith and less on penance than Aquinas does. This and other differences will become significant when we attempt to understand the behavior of the hero in Shakespeare's repentance plays. But the important fact is that Shakespeare used repentance as a plot device throughout his career, and finally worked his way to a dramatic form adequate to a serious treatment of repentance as a means to salvation of personal integrity in this world and presumably to salvation of man's immortal soul in the world to come.

---

4. Cf. Robert Hunter, *Shakespeare and the Comedy of Foregiveness* (New York, 1965), p. 169, and *Cymbeline*, ed. J. M. Nosworthy (London, 1955), p. 162 n.
5. Hart, *passim.*

Shakespeare's Repentance Plays

1
Repentance
in Shakespeare's Complication Comedies

T HE earliest of Shakespeare's comedies to make extensive use of the doctrine of repentance are *The Two Gentlemen of Verona, Much Ado about Nothing* and *All's Well that Ends Well.* But, because of the nature of the plays, all three deal with it superficially. Structurally, they are what may be called complication comedies: the emphasis is on the plot, which is built around a central complication. Shakespeare got the form, either directly or indirectly, from the Roman New Comedy of Plautus and Terence.[1]

In Roman New Comedy the complication is usually the set of circumstances that keeps a pair of lovers apart. Terence's *Andria* is typical: a boy wants to marry a girl, but his father objects to the girl's low birth. The father insists that the boy marry the daughter of the father's best friend instead. The boy, aided by his slave, tries a number of schemes to outwit the father. The schemes fail, and the lovers' cause seems lost when suddenly it turns out that the

---

1. See T. W. Baldwin, *William Shakespeare's Five Act Structure* (Urbana, Ill., 1947). Baldwin discusses at great length Shakespeare's debt to Terence and the possible ways in which Shakespeare may have known him. There is evidence that Shakespeare knew Plautus at firsthand. *The Comedy of Errors* is an adaptation of Plautus' *Menaechmi*, to which elements from *Amphitruo*, also by Plautus, have been added. Aside from *Errors*, the play that shows the Plautine influence most strongly is *Twelfth Night.*

girl is not low born after all—she is the long-lost daughter of the father's friend.

The structure of *Andria* is very simple. Boy wants girl, but boy is kept from girl by a complication—the father's insistence that the boy marry someone else. The main interest in the play lies in the deceptions used by the lovers to outwit the father. Character development and realistic situation are of far less importance than the twists and turns of plot and the cleverness of the intrigue. There is no important philosophical theme.

Although the plots of most Roman New Comedies are based on a boy-wants-girl situation, the plays are virtually never romantic or sentimental. The lovers are seldom attractive; the boy is often a whimpering fool, and the girl is usually faceless. Nor do the plays necessarily end in marriage. In *Pseudolus, Asinaria,* and *Curculio,* for example, the plot revolves around the attempt of a young man to swindle a courtesan away from a *leno* (white slaver). Sometimes the boy-girl plot forms the skeletal structure of the play but does not receive the main emphasis. In *Miles Gloriosus,* for instance, the focus of the play is on the gulling of an intolerable knave.[2]

All of Shakespeare's Elizabethan comedies—from *The Comedy of Errors* (c. 1592) to *All's Well that Ends Well* (c. 1602-1603)[3]—are complication comedies. Shakespeare is far more romantic and sentimental than Plautus and Terence, but his comedies are similar in structure to theirs. The development of the plot—that is, the setting up and resolving of the central complication—is of paramount importance.

---

2. Plautus has quite a few plays in which the emphasis is on comic elements rather than love plot: *e.g., Asinaria, Aulularia, Bacchides.*

3. Dates from E. K. Chambers, *William Shakespeare, A Study of Facts and Problems* (Oxford, 1930).

Except in *The Comedy of Errors,* an adaption of Plautus's *Menaechmi,* Shakespeare's complication comedies always involve the temporary separation of lovers. The principle on which all these plays are constructed is that the course of true love never runs smooth until the fifth act.

On the surface of these plays there is a good deal of discussion of philosophical themes, but the themes are not integral to the plots, and do not govern them. We may see this clearly in Shakespeare's first play to use the theme of sin and repentance, *The Two Gentlemen of Verona.* *Two Gentlemen* is based on the tale of Felismena, an incident in Jorge de Montemayor's romance, *Diana Enamorada.* The plot may be summarized briefly: Felix woos Felismena, who accepts him as her lover, and they enjoy a brief period of happiness before Felix's father sends him to the court of the empress. Felismena follows Felix to court disguised as a boy. She overhears him serenading a new love, Celia, and realizes that Felix has betrayed her. The disguised Felismena becomes Felix's page, and he sends her to woo Celia in his behalf. Celia falls in love with the page, and when Felismena does not return her love, Celia dies of a broken heart. Crushed by Celia's death, Felix disappears from court. Felismena sets out in pursuit. She finds Felix; he repents his infidelity, and they marry.

Shakespeare converts Montemayor's tale into a complication comedy on the Roman model. He sets up the intrigue by adding a second gentleman, Valentine. There is no intrigue in Montemayor's tale; Felix simply forsakes Felismena for Celia. In *Two Gentlemen,* Proteus intrigues against Valentine in order to steal Silvia. To emphasize the intrigue, Shakespeare shifts the primary focus of the play to the two gentlemen, in contrast to Montemayor's focus on Felismena, the first-person narrator.

The addition of Valentine provides Celia's counterpart, Silvia, with a suitable lover, and spares her Celia's cruel fate—a broken heart. With two pairs of lovers, Shakespeare has the makings of a happy ending for all the major characters. Apart from these differences, he follows Montemayor closely.

The last scene of the play involves Shakespeare's first, and perhaps least effective, use of repentance. Silvia, who has run away from her father's court in search of the banished Valentine, is overtaken by Proteus. He pleads for her love, and when his wooing fails to move her, he assaults her. Fortunately Valentine is nearby, and he leaps out of the bushes to save Silvia. Proteus repents his villainy, and begs forgiveness of Valentine, who not only forgives Proteus but offers him Silvia. Just then Julia, who has been watching these goings-on disguised as Proteus's page, reveals her identity. Proteus decides to take Julia instead of Silvia. Valentine reclaims Silvia, and the play ends happily with plans for a double marriage.

The play is not one of Shakespeare's best, but it has been appreciated even less than it deserves because it has been misunderstood. The critics' chief complaint is that it is unrealistic. They object especially to the ending, in which Proteus and Valentine exchange Silvia back and forth. E. K. Chambers says:

> One realizes that tragicomedy must have its reconciliation; but surely this is a reconciliation, in its almost cynical brevity and lack of psychology, to leave one gasping.[4]

Until recently, Shakespeare's defenders have limited themselves to arguing that either the text is corrupt or

---

4. *Shakespeare: A Survey* (London, 1925), p. 51.

the meaning is ambiguous.[5] In a recent book, however, Robert Hunter argues that the ending is psychologically realistic, according to Elizabethan lights.[6] He contends that Proteus repents his sinful deeds and convinces Valentine that he is truly contrite. (Nothing, Hunter observes, is more conducive to contrition than getting caught.) Valentine pardons Proteus because forgiveness is a Christian duty. In short, Hunter's point is that, although Valentine's actions are incomprehensible by modern standards of behavior, they would have seemed both convincing and laudable to Shakespeare's devout Elizabethan audience.

Hunter's argument that the concept of sin and repentance is being used seriously as a theme of *Two Gentlemen* rests on his conclusion that Proteus's repentance is to be taken seriously as a revelation of character. It can be demonstrated, however, that Proteus's repentance is merely a superficial plot device.

In order to make his point about repentance, Hunter cites Proteus's repentance speech, and Valentine's answer:

> Pro.   My shame and guilt confounds me.
>   Forgive me, Valentine; if hearty sorrow
>   Be a sufficient ransom for offence,
>   I tender't here; I do as truly suffer,
>   As e'er I did commit.
>
> Val.   Then I am paid;
>   And once again I do receive thee honest.

---

5. Warwick Bond, the Arden editor, advances the theory of a Dr. Batteston, otherwise unidentified, who argues that Shakespeare is being deliberately ambiguous—that Valentine is offering Proteus only an equal share in his heart with Silvia, not possession of her. (Arden *Two Gentlemen*, xxxvii.) In a footnote on the same page Bond hesitantly advances his reading of the lines: "All the love that devotion to Silvia lets me call my own, I give to thee."

6. *Shakespeare and the Comedy of Forgiveness* (New York, 1965), pp. 86–87.

> Who by repentance is not satisfied
> Is nor of heaven nor earth, for these are pleas'd.
> By penitence the Eternal's wrath's appeas'd.
>
> V, iv, 73–81[7]

This is certainly the rhetoric of repentance, and it is Shakespeare's addition. It is not in Montemayor's story. Felix asks forgiveness of Felismena, but only as an unfaithful lover. Felix does not repent to appease the Eternal, or to save his soul.

Despite his use of the rhetoric of repentance, Proteus is hardly convincing. The Homily "Of Repentance" says that a true repentance is accompanied by "fasting, weeping and mourning, these penitential acts being necessary as an admission that we deserve punishment at the hands of God."[8] It may be argued that drama demands compression, and can only suggest these actions; yet one need only compare Shakespeare's dramatic treatment of the repentance of Leontes in *The Winter's Tale,* or that of Posthumus in *Cymbeline,* to see that Proteus's repentance is pretty much a *pro forma* affair.

In *The Winter's Tale* Leontes submits himself to sixteen years of penitential self-humiliation, a "saint-like sorrow," as it is described by one of his lords. Though the period of Posthumus's contrition is shorter, his self-abasement in *Cymbeline* is as thoroughgoing as that of Leontes. Posthumus welcomes imprisonment: "Must I repent, I cannot do it better than in gyves" (V, iv, 14).

Compared with the somber tone of the dramatic presentation of the atonement of Leontes and Posthumus, the scene of Proteus's repentance has almost a carnival air.

---

7. All quotations from Shakespeare in this book are taken from the New Cambridge Edition of Shakespeare's works, ed. W. A. Neilson and C. J. Hill (Cambridge, Mass., 1942).

8. P. 530.

Proteus states simply that he is ashamed of his conduct and sorry for it. Valentine answers that he is satisfied by this repentance and, in order to show Proteus that all is forgiven, offers him Silvia. There is nothing ambiguous about Valentine's statement:

> And, that my love may appear plain and free,
> All that was mine in Silvia I give thee.
> V, iv, 82–85.

It means simply, "As a proof of my love, Proteus, I give you Silvia." Whatever one's ideas of Christian duty, this is certainly a strange act of supererogation.

The scene should be understood in the light of the demands of the Plautine and Terentian plot structure. There are two pairs of lovers in the double plot of *Two Gentlemen;* the knot of the complication is tied when one lover forsakes his mistress and woos the other's lady. In order to solve the complication, the fickle lover must change his mind again and take back his former love.

A sudden change of mind that brings about the denouement is a New Comedy plot device, a comic analogue of the *deus ex machina* of classical tragedy.[9] To make the dramatic manipulation seem less contrived, Shakespeare uses the rhetoric of repentance to cloak Proteus's turnabout with the appearance of an orthodox Christian repentance. Although the scene is not supposed to be realistic in the modern sense of the term, Valentine's forgiveness of Proteus was understandable to an Elizabethan audience in terms of ideal if not actual human behavior.

---

9. I am indebted for the idea about the analogy of the sudden change of mood in comedy and the *deus ex machina* of tragedy to H. J. Rose, who makes the comparison in describing the denouement of Plautus' *Mostellaria* in *A Handbook of Latin Literature* (Dutton Paperback, New York, 1960), p. 50.

As for the "Silvia offer," Valentine's proposed transfer to Proteus of his proprietary interest in Silvia seems by today's standards, the act of a "heel," not that of a romantic hero. It may also be explained, however, in terms of Elizabethan ideals of behavior. The surrender of a fiancée to a friend is a motif that recurs in medieval and Renaissance literature.[10] Although one suspects that this sort of friendly act was rarer in life than in art, the theme of a friendship stronger than love was at least a literary ideal of behavior, and Shakespeare makes use of it to give some appearance of reality to his final dramatic manipulation in *Two Gentlemen*. Valentine's offer of Silvia to Proteus is the last twist in the plot, the last snarl to be untangled in the knot of the complication. In the plays of Plautus and Terence the action is busy up until the final moment, and the outcome is in doubt until the very end. Valentine's offer presents a final problem to be solved before the lovers can be correctly paired off for mating and all can end well.

In *Two Gentlemen*, Shakespeare disguises the bare frame of the intrigue plot by covering it with the drapery of two familiar concepts: the Christian doctrine of forgiveness, and the classical ideal of friendship between men. The action of the play, which has puzzled critics for years, may be understood if we recognize that Shakespeare is using the intrigue plot of Roman New Comedy and adapting this structure to his needs by making the actions of his characters understandable in terms of Elizabethan ideals of behavior.

Understanding, however, does not insure approval, and seeing what Shakespeare is about in *Two Gentlemen* only

10. See *Two Gentlemen*, ed. Warwick Bond (Arden Edition, London, 1903), p. xxi.

makes it clear that Chambers was instinctively right in his disapproval of the ending. Even though we understand Elizabethan standards of judgment, and we grant that Shakespeare ascribes plausible motives to the actions of his characters, the ending of any play is successful only if it is emotionally satisfying to the audience. Comedy, like all drama, arouses emotional expectations in those who view it. In the comedies of Plautus, Terence, and Shakespeare the audience sympathizes with the lovers and despises those who keep them apart. A successful ending to a complication comedy must be a happy one—that is, one in which the sympathetic characters prevail, and the hostile characters are either punished or made to recant publicly. In *The Merchant of Venice,* for instance, Shylock is crushed, and the lovers triumph. This ending, we may be sure, was satisfying to virtually every member of Shakespeare's original audience. It was not until fairly recently that people sympathized with Shylock as a member of a persecuted minority group. In one respect *The Merchant* uses the simplest form of the New Comedy pattern: a villain threatens the happiness of the lovers. In the denouement, the villain is defeated, and the threat removed.

The pattern is more complex in *Two Gentlemen:* Proteus, the villain, is also one of the lovers. He cannot simply be defeated; he must also repent, be forgiven, and be married off. Since both the man he betrays and the woman he forsakes forgive him, there should be no problem. But there is one: Julia loves Proteus, Valentine is his friend, and so perhaps both can be expected to forgive Proteus easily. The audience has been conditioned to despise Proteus, and so is less willing to let him off. This reluctance is felt whether or not one believes in the Christian duty of forgiveness. Most Elizabethans would have been aware that the Homily "Of Repentance" describes fasting and weeping as signs of a true repentance, and it is possible that they did not take much more kindly to Proteus than we do. Critics have raised fewer outcries about the happy fates reserved for Posthumus and Leontes, who achieve their pardons (as far as this is theologically possible), than they have about Proteus, Claudio (*Much Ado*), Bertram (*All's Well*), and Angelo (*Measure for Measure*), who seemingly have their pardons thrust upon them.

Like *Two Gentlemen, Much Ado about Nothing* is an intrigue comedy. In it, as in *Two Gentlemen,* Shakespeare makes use of the theme of sin and repentance. Once again, he uses it superficially.

In *Much Ado* Claudio shamefully jilts his fiancée, Hero, at the altar. When he realizes that he has acted wrongfully, he repents the sin as a Christian. The source of the Hero-Claudio plot, the story of the wronged fiancée, appeared in a number of versions during the sixteenth century. The one that corresponds most closely to Shakespeare's is Matteo Bandello's Twenty-second Novella.[11] The story may be summarized briefly: Timbreo loves Finecia. His friend Girondo becomes jealous and plots against him. Girondo persuades Timbreo to watch Finecia's house one night. Timbreo sees a man climb a ladder and enter a window. Believing that Finecia has betrayed him, Timbreo jilts her. The girl swoons, and her parents spread the story that she has died. Soon both Timbreo and Girondo regret their actions. Girondo confesses to Timbreo how he deceived him; he had arranged to have a man climb into an unused bedroom and the man had not been near Finecia. Timbreo pardons

---

11. No Elizabethan English translation of Bandello is known. Shakespeare may have used Belleforest's French translation. See Geoffrey Bullough, *Narrative and Dramatic Sources of Shakespeare* (New York, 1958), 2: 65, 66.

his friend, and both beg forgiveness of the girl's parents. They are pardoned on the condition that Timbreo allow Finecia's father to choose Timbreo's wife. Timbreo agrees, and finds that his new bride is Finecia.

The story as it stands possesses all the elements of an intrigue comedy: the two lovers, Timbreo and Finecia; the intriguer, Girondo; and the complication—the blot on Finecia's chastity—that keeps the lovers from marrying.

Much Ado incorporates much of Bandello's tale. Timbreo and Finecia become Hero and Claudio. Girondo becomes Don John, the villainous intriguer. John, like Girondo, uses a "window trick" to dupe his victim. Claudio, like Timbreo, falls for the deception and jilts his fiancée. Shakespeare makes the jilting more dramatic by having it take place at the altar.

Claudio's rejection of Hero is clearly sinful by Elizabethan standards, which held that it is a man's moral duty to make sure that he is right before making a judgment. And it cannot be pleaded in Claudio's defense that he is simply making an honest mistake. Even though Shakespeare's addition of the maid, Margaret, makes the deception more convincing, Claudio is duty bound, by Elizabethan precepts, to use his reason so as to avoid falling into this kind of error. As Richard Hooker says:

> There is not that good which concerneth us, but it hath evidence for itself, if Reason were diligent to search it out. Through neglect thereof, abused we are with the show of that which is not; sometimes the subtility of Satan inveigling us as it did Eve, sometimes the hastiness of our wills preventing the more considerate advice of sound Reason.[12]

Claudio sins both because he is inveigled by the subtlety of

---

12. *Of the Laws of Ecclesiastical Polity* (Oxford, 1896), I, vii, 7.

Don John, and because he acts too hastily upon the urging
of his wrath, without making further investigation of
Hero's supposed guilt.

When Claudio discovers that Hero is innocent, he repents. He tells Hero's father Leonato

> Impose me to what penance your invention
> Can lay upon my sin . . .
> > V, i, 283, 284

Leonato stipulates that Claudio

> Hang her an epitath upon her tomb
> And sing it to her bones. . .
> > V, ii, 294–95

Leonato further requests that, since Claudio cannot marry
Hero, he marry instead his niece, a girl who is "almost the
copy of my child that's dead."

Claudio willingly undertakes this penance. He goes to
the church in which he believes Hero is buried, and over
what he supposes to be her grave he sings:

> "Pardon, goddess of the night,
> Those that slew thy virgin knight;
> For the which, with songs of woe,
> Round about her tomb they go."
> > V, iii, 12–15

He promises to repeat this rite yearly. Then he goes to
Leonato's house to meet his bride. The girl, of course,
turns out to be Hero.

But there is a good deal to *Much Ado* besides the Hero-
Claudio plot. Viewers remember the battles of Beatrice and
Benedick, and the foolery of Dogberry and Verges, Shake-
speare's own inventions, long after they have forgotten

Hero and Claudio. In Roman New Comedy a love story may serve as the frame for a play in which a comic subplot provides the main interest—we have noted *Miles Gloriosus* as an obvious example. Shakespeare follows this pattern in *Much Ado*. The Hero-Claudio love plot gives the play its skeletal structure, but the battle of wits between Beatrice and Benedick and the clowning of Dogberry and Verges are the flesh and blood. The play is a light-hearted comedy with a few melodramatic moments, chief of these being the jilting of Hero. The title of the play indicates that we are not to take this too seriously.

In short, although sin and repentance play a part in *Much Ado*, here, as in *Two Gentlemen*, it is primarily the means to a happy ending. Once again, it is far less important than it is in *Measure for Measure, Cymbeline,* and *The Winter's Tale*.

Most critics consider *All's Well That Ends Well* a different type of play from Shakespeare's previous comedies. They group it with *Measure for Measure* and *Troilus and Cressida*, describing the three as "problem plays." W. W. Lawrence, who is largely responsible for popularizing the term, says

> The essential characteristic of a problem play . . . is that a perplexing and distressing complication in human life is presented in a spirit of high seriousness. This special treatment distinguishes such a play from other kinds of drama, in that the theme is handled so as to arouse not merely interest or excitement, or pity or amusement, but to probe the complicated interrelations of character and action, in a situation admitting of different ethical interpretations.[13]

This description, as we will see in the next chapter, fits

---

13. *Shakespeare's Problem Comedies* (New York, 1931), p. 4.

Measure for Measure but not *All's Well That Ends Well*.
All's Well, like Shakespeare's previous comedies, is a complication comedy. The theme does not probe the interrelations of character and action; it merely gives an appearance
of realism to an artificial plot. The tone is a little darker
than it is in some of Shakespeare's earlier comedies, but
the structure is the same. Shakespeare follows his established procedure of taking a familiar tale and fitting it
into the intrigue-comedy pattern.

Shakespeare's source for *All's Well* is Boccaccio's tale
of Giletta of Narbona. In Boccaccio's tale, Giletta, the
daughter of a physician, cures the King of France of an
illness believed incurable. The King rewards her by letting
her choose a husband from among the nobles of the realm.
The girl chooses Beltramo, the son of her father's former
lord. Beltramo objects to the girl's low birth, but on the
King's insistence marries her. He then leaves for the wars
without consummating the marriage, telling his wife he will
not live with her until she performs two seemingly impossible tasks: getting his ring from his finger and bearing
a son by him without his cooperation. Giletta follows her
husband into Italy, and slips into bed with him when he
thinks he is seducing someone else. She gets the ring, and
nine months later bears him two sons. When Beltramo sees
that his demands are met, he becomes a loving husband.

Boccaccio's tale is based on a familiar folktale motif,
the fulfillment of tasks. Lawrence, who cites a number of
analogues to the tale, describes the motif as follows:

A wife is deserted by her husband, to be taken back on the ful-
filment of apparently impossible conditions, one of which is to get
a child by him. She performs these tasks, and wins back her
husband.[14]

14. *Ibid.,* p. 41.

The standard elements of this type of tale are a reluctant bridegroom, a "clever wench," and a set of seemingly impossible demands. When the demands are met, the husband always returns to his wife and a happy marriage.

The tale fits easily into the complication comedy pattern. There is the necessary pair of eligible young people. The seemingly impossible tasks serve as the complication to keep them apart, and the clever wench acts as the intriguer.

In adapting the tale for the stage, the dramatist must provide the appearance of plausible motivation for the characters. In the tale, Beltramo has a complete change of heart toward the wife he has scorned when she fulfills his demands by tricking him. This sort of inexplicable behavior is perfectly acceptable in a narrative with strong folktale elements. When the tale is put on the stage, however, it comes to life, and the characters must appear to act on understandable motives. Shakespeare finds a solution in the theme of sin and repentance. He provides Bertram with clear motives for his reluctance to marry and for his desertion of his wife. He makes it clear that this desertion is sinful. At the end of the play, Shakespeare ties Bertram's reconciliation with his wife to his repentance.

In Boccaccio's story, as in most "clever wench" tales, the wife who is of lower birth proves herself worthy of her husband's love by fulfilling the demands he sets her. As Hunter points out, Shakespeare makes a fundamental alteration in the story by blackening the character of Bertram and making him a sinner in need of regeneration and forgiveness. Now "instead of a clever wench who must prove herself worthy of an aristocratic husband, we have an unworthy husband who must be made worthy of his wife."[15]

Bertram's sin is disobedience to his king, who has told Helena:

---

15. *Shakespeare and the Comedy of Forgiveness*, p. 112.

> . . . Make choice and see,
> Who shuns thy love shuns all his love in me.
>
> II, ii, 78–79

Helena chooses Bertram, and he shuns her love on the
grounds that she is too low born for him. The King replies
that nobility is a matter of virtue, not title, but that if
Bertram is disturbed about Helena's low rank, he will raise
it. Bertram remains adamant:

> I cannot love her, nor will strive to do't.
>
> II, ii, 152

The King makes it clear that Bertram's refusal is a rebuke
to him, the King, as well as to Helena.

> My honour's at the stake; which to defeat,
> I must produce my power.
>
> II, iii, 156–57

He orders Bertram:

> . . . Check thy contempt;
> Obey our will, which travails in thy good;
> . . . As thou lov'st her,
> Thy love's to me religious; else, does err.
>
> II, iii, 164, 165; 189, 190

From a modern point of view, the King may seem wrong
in forcing Bertram to marry against his will, and Bertram
may seem justified in deserting Helena. But an Elizabethan
audience would have felt the King's actions proper because
of his obviously superior perception of Helena's merits.
Helena is a sympathetic character; Bertram is despicable
in his disdain for her. And Bertram flouts the King by
deserting Helena. He runs away without even consummating his marriage. He tells Parolles:

> Although before the solemn priest I have sworn,
> I will not bed her.
>
> > II, iii, 286, 287

He tells Helena:

> When thou canst get the ring upon my finger
> which never shall come off, and show me a
> child begotten of thy body that I am father
> to, then call me husband; but in such a "then"
> I write a "never."
>
> > III, ii, 59–63

These conditions are the complication in the play. Usually the complication keeps lovers from marrying; here it keeps a man and wife from consummating their marriage. Shakespeare had used this variation earlier in *The Merchant of Venice*: Bassanio and Portia cannot consummate their marriage until they rescue Antonio from Shylock.

Helena is the intriguer in the play. She follows Bertram to Italy, where she finds that he has been trying to seduce a young girl named Diana. Helena persuades Diana to agree to an assignation with Bertram, and arranges to take the girl's place in bed. A number of critics have been offended by the indelicacy of Helena's action. But Bertram is her husband, after all, and traditionally the clever wench is deemed justified in tricking her husband into bed. Helena seems justified in defending her conduct as having "lawful meaning in a lawful act." Bertram's conduct, however, is sinful. Helena describes it as "wicked meaning in a lawful deed." That is, although it is a lawful deed to lie with one's wife, Bertram's intention—adultery—is sinful. So, although Helena is justified in sleeping with Bertram, Bertram sins in sleeping with Helena.

Bertram brazens it out to the end, repenting his sins

only after he is caught. When Diana arrives at court and accuses Bertram of seducing and abandoning her, he attempts to lie his way out of the predicament by accusing the girl of being a camp follower. The girl, Diana, will not give the King a straightforward account of what happens; she speaks only in riddles:

> Because he's guilty, and he is not guilty:
> He knows I am no maid, and he'll swear to't:
> I'll swear I am a maid, and he knows not.
>   V, iii, 290–92

The situation is confused until Helena arrives and confronts Bertram. He is overwhelmed by his guilt, and exclaims.

> O, pardon!
> V, iii, 309

Helena forgives him, and explains what has happened. All ends well as the two plan to live together henceforth.

Bertram's repentance is even more perfunctory than that of Proteus or Claudio. All that we hear him say is the startled exclamation "O, pardon!" It seems clear that what we have here is not the serious examination of the problems of human behavior that takes place in the other "problem plays," *Measure for Measure* and *Troilus and Cressida,* but rather the typical bewildering denouement of complication comedy, in which the emphasis is on wringing the last bit of suspense out of the plot. This is the purpose of Diana's riddles. Giving important information in riddles is a common feature of folktale. Shakespeare uses it here as a final snarl in the knot of the complication.

In other words, in order to give his highly artificial

plot a veneer of reality, Shakespeare presents Bertram's actions in terms of sin and repentance. Bertram's reluctance to marry Helena, and his desertion of her afterwards, are made to appear the sins of a wayward youth. His reconciliation with Helena comes as a result of his repentance. In arguing that repentance is treated seriously in *All's Well*,[16] Hunter is simply going beyond the evidence.

To sum up, Shakespeare's Elizabethan comedies are complication comedies—plays about love with contrived plots that use last-minute reversals to bring separated lovers together. In *Two Gentlemen, Much Ado,* and *All's Well,* the lovers are kept apart by the hero's sinful rejection of the heroine's love. Hero and heroine are brought together at the denouement when the hero repents, and the heroine forgives him. Shakespeare uses the doctrine of repentance in these plays only to give an air of plausibility to the hero's last-minute change of heart and to bring the play to a happy ending. Such manipulation of a serious religious doctrine for the dramatist's convenience is acceptable only because the audience, viewing a complication comedy, expects a happy ending and therefore accepts it uncritically. Furthermore, no real attention is paid to the deeper emotions of the characters involved or to the moral basis of their actions. Serious attention to character portrayal and particularly to the moral basis of conduct would demand a far more careful delineation of repentance if it were to be accepted by the audience. But such delineation would also require a different kind of plot from the facile intrigues of complication comedy. Toward such plots Shakespeare worked his way as he moved on to probe human motives more deeply.

---

16. *Ibid.,* p. 131.

2

Measure for Measure:
Shakespeare's First Serious Treatment
of Repentance

MEASURE for Measure marks a new departure
in Shakespearean comedy. It is a far more serious
play than the complication comedies with their emphasis on
plot. In *Measure for Measure* the emphasis is on the
theme of sin and repentance, and for the first time Shakespeare examines repentance in depth. To use Lawrence's
phrase, he handles the theme "so as to probe the com-
plicated interrelations of character and action" in human
behavior. In this respect *Measure for Measure,* which was
written in the same three- or four-year span as *Othello,
Hamlet,* and *King Lear,* is closer to Shakespeare's tragedies
than it is to his Elizabethan comedies. As Virgil Whitaker
puts it, Shakespeare applies to *Measure for Measure* the
"same philosophical analysis of human action that he employed in writing the mature tragedies."[1]

Shakespeare's tragedies explore the effects of sin on
the noblest men of their times. The emphasis in the plays
is on the psychology of sin. There is a key scene in each

---

1. "Philosophy and Romance in Shakespeare's 'Problem' Comedies," *The
Seventeenth Century: Studies in the History of English Thought and
Literature from Bacon to Pope* (Stanford, 1951), p. 339.

tragedy in which the hero faces a difficult moral choice. Except possibly for Hamlet, he invariably lets his passions overrule his reason, and sins. Brutus decides to join the conspirators in assassinating Caesar; Othello decides to kill Desdemona; Lear disinherits Cordelia and banishes Kent; Macbeth decides to murder Duncan. In each scene the hero's mental processes are depicted in detail in accordance with Elizabethan psychology. After these scenes of moral choice, the hero goes on to commit his fatal act, and the rest of the play chronicles his decline and fall.[2]

Several of the tragedies treat the possibility of repentance. Hamlet pleads with his mother to repent her sins (in the "closet scene", III, iv). In the same play Claudius attempts to repent in a prayer scene that parallels exactly the points in the Homily, but he fails because he cannot bear to give up the things his sins have brought him, his wife and kingdom (III, iii).[3] In *Macbeth,* Cawdor repents his treason against Duncan (I, iv). In doing so, he provides a contrast to Macbeth, who dies unrepentant, in despair. Virgil Whitaker argues that Lear's repentance is completed when he is finally reunited with Cordelia.[4] If, however, Lear does repent his treatment of Cordelia, he is the only one of Shakespeare's tragic heroes to undergo a complete repentance in the Homily's terms. The others die unrepentant, for Othello acknowledges only his error, and speaks specifically of his damnation:

---

2. For a full discussion of Shakespeare's tragedies of moral choice see Virgil Whitaker, *Shakespeare's Use of Learning* (San Marino, 1964), chaps. 10, 12.

3. Eleanor Prosser argues that Hamlet repents killing Polonius, and thereby has "apparently checked his own descent into Hell." (*Hamlet and Revenge* [Stanford, Calif., 1967] p. 217). But, as Miss Prosser admits, there is a good deal of evidence that Hamlet is not repentant. See, for instance, his remarks to Horatio about killing Rosencrantz and Guildenstern (V, ii).

4. *The Mirror up to Nature* (San Marino, 1965), p. 224.

> O ill-starr'd wench!
> Pale as thy smock! When we shall meet at compt,
> This look of thine will hurl my soul from heaven,
> And fiends will snatch at it.
>
> V, ii, 272–75

Like the tragedies, *Measure for Measure* is based on moral choice. Here the pattern is clearly twofold: the hero, Angelo, not only sins and falls, but repents and is redeemed. Angelo's sin and repentance provide one major theme of the play. Other important themes deal with the particular sins themselves, lechery and the improper use of power by a ruler. Angelo sins in attempting to commit fornication with Isabella, and in condemning a man to death for a crime that he, too, has committed. Shakespeare explores the theme of lechery from a number of angles. In addition to Angelo, Claudio and Lucio and Mistress Overdone and her crew are guilty of sins ranging from fornication to prostitution and pandering.

In the tragedies Shakespeare has a dramatic form capable of dealing with serious themes. In *Measure for Measure* he retains the form he used in his complication comedies, which is poorly suited for a serious theme. Consequently, *Measure for Measure,* despite—or perhaps because of— the careful delineation of character, is weak dramatically. The ensuing discussion of the play will be devoted to supporting these observations.

Shakespeare gets from his sources the story of *Measure for Measure* and the major theme of the play, sin and repentance, as well as the ancillary themes, lechery and the abuse of power. The sources were Geraldi Cinthio's novella *Epitia*[5] and George Whetstone's ten-act comedy *Pro-*

---

5. Hecattommithi, Decade 8, Novella 5. For convenience' sake I will refer to the tale as *Epitia*. According to Bullough *Promos and Cassandra* was Shakespeare's chief source, but he probably used *Epitia* as well.

mos and Cassandra, based on Cinthio's novella. Both
emphasize ethical problems and moral choice, and so differ
from the love tales that serve as the sources of most of the
Elizabethan comedies. Shakespeare's choice of sources is
one indication of the direction he intends his comedy to
take.

Cinthio's novella is based on a folktale motif that appears in many forms during the Middle Ages and early
Renaissance, one that the critics, following Mary Lascelles,
have called the "monstrous ransom,"[6] but that I prefer
more specifically to call the sexual ransom.

In such tales, a girl is asked to rescue someone dear to
her—a brother or husband—by giving herself to the judge
or creditor who has the loved one in his power. In Cinthio's
novella the ruler of Innsbruck condemns Vico, a young
man, to death for raping a virgin. Vico's sister, Epitia,
pleads with Juriste to spare her brother's life. She argues
that Vico was motivated by his love for the girl, and that
he is willing to marry her. Juriste is moved more by Epitia's
beauty than by her arguments, and he offers to spare Vico
if Epitia will lie with him. Epitia at first spurns Juriste's
advances, but when her brother begs her to save him, she
submits. Juriste betrays his bargain and has Vico beheaded.
Epitia tells her story to the Emperor, who forces Juriste
to marry Epitia to restore her reputation, then orders
Juriste beheaded. Epitia begs the Emperor to spare the
life of her new husband. The Emperor does, and the
couple lives happily ever after.

In this strongly didactic tale Cinthio deals with two
main themes, love and justice. He makes two main points
about justice. First, the law is inviolate; the most serious
crime a ruler can commit against his people is to tamper

6. *Measure for Measure* (London, 1953), p. 7.

with the law to gratify his own desires. When the Emperor installs Juriste as ruler of Innsbruck, he charges him: "Keep justice inviolate, even if you have to give sentence against me who am your overlord. I could forgive you all other faults but anything done against justice. . . ."[7] Second, Cinthio shows that the highest form of justice is that in which the judge tempers the strict administration of the law with mercy. In pleading for Juriste's life, Epitia argues, "Clemency makes a monarch most like the Immortal Gods."[8] The Emperor, convinced, pardons Juriste.

Although the Christian ethic is implicit in Epitia's remarks about justice and mercy, Cinthio is concerned only with civil law—with the pardon of Juriste as an offender against the state, not with the fate of Juriste as a repentant sinner who will be judged by God.

Concerning love, Cinthio makes a distinction between fornication committed in the heat of ardent love, and that done for lust. In pleading for her brother Epitia argues that

> if the law might be alleviated in any case, it should be in offenses done for love, especially where the honor of the injured lady remained unharmed, as it would in her brother's case, who was very willing to make her his wife.[9]

Vico's action, though sinful, is far less so than that of Juriste in forcing Epitia to submit. Cinthio states that Juriste's attraction for Epitia is "lustful desire." Unlike Vico, Juriste has no intention of marrying the woman he seduces.

Epitia's willingness to sacrifice her virginity to save her brother, and her loyalty to her husband when he is threat-

---

7. Bullough, *Sources,* 2: 429.
8. *Ibid.,* p. 429.
9. *Ibid.,* p. 422.

ened with execution, are treated as models of sororal and conjugal love.

George Whetstone follows Cinthio's story closely, but his *Promos and Cassandra* broadens Cinthio's theme by introducing the element of divine judgment of the sinner. Promos, the ruler of Julio, a city in Hungary, condemns a youth, Andrugio, to death for having premarital intercourse with his fiancée, Polina. Andrugio's sister, Cassandra, pleads with Promos to spare the youth's life. Promos, urged on by his evil counselor Phallax, proposes the sexual ransom—Cassandra's virginity for Andrugio's life. Cassandra agrees, but after possessing her Promos betrays her. He orders the jailer to execute Andrugio and to send his head to Cassandra. However, the sympathetic jailer disobeys Promos's order. He frees Andrugio, and sends Cassandra the head of a recently executed felon. Cassandra, deceived, tells the King about her bargain with Promos. The King makes Promos marry Cassandra, and then condemns him to death. While in jail Promos repents his sin. He begs Cassandra and others whom he has injured to forgive him, and he asks them to pray that God, too, will forgive him. Cassandra pleads for Promos's life, but the King's officer tells her that the law demands a life for a life—that Promos must pay for Andrugio's death with his own. At this point Andrugio steps forward, and the King pardons Promos and restores him to power as ruler of Julio.

Whetstone has taken a moral tale, dramatized it in accordance with classical ideas of comedy,[10] and incorporated

---

10. Whetstone cites the plays of Menander, Plautus, and Terence as his models of dramatic form (Bullough, *Sources,* 2: 443). It is probable that he changed Cinthio's story, sparing the life of the heroine's brother, because he felt, with the New Comedy poets, that death is too serious a subject for comedy.

elements from a contemporary didactic dramatic form, the ruler morality play.[11] The result is a comedy that examines serious themes. The first is the responsibility of the Christian ruler to his subjects and to God. The play argues, specifically, that the interests of the state are best served if, in judging a good man who has broken the law, legality is tempered with mercy. This is the principle that guides the King in pardoning Promos and restoring him to power. If, on the other hand, the ruler abuses his power, he commits not only a civil crime, but sins against God as well.

A second theme deals with the sin of lechery. Whetstone makes the same distinction as Cinthio. Fornication committed because of the "blynde affects" of love is sinful, but far less so than that motivated by lust—Andrugio's sin is less serious than Promos's. Cassandra, like her counterpart, Epitia, shows ideal sororal and conjugal love.

In the last act Promos repents his sins and prays to God

---

11. Ruler morality plays like John Skelton's *Magnificence* and David Lindsay's *Ane Satyre of the Thrie Estaitis* have plots similar to that of *Epitia*. In *Magnificence*, for instance, a model ruler, Magnificence, is corrupted by evil counselors and becomes dissolute and tyrannical. He is punished by Adversity, the scourge of God, and stripped of his powers. When Magnificence repents, Good Hope and Redress restore him to power. The central plot of *Thrie Estaitis* is much the same. Whetstone borrows a number of dramatic conventions from these plays in dramatizing *Epitia*. Specifically, the chief points of similarity between *Promos and Cassandra* and the ruler plays are as follows: 1. Structure: the narrative pattern of Cinthio's tale already matches the tragicomic structural pattern of the ruler plays, but it should be noted that like the ruler of the moral plays Promos is restored to power at the denouement of *Promos and Cassandra*. In *Epitia* Juriste is merely pardoned and dismissed to live happily ever after with his wife. 2. Theme: Whetstone adopts the moral play theme of sin and repentance; he combines Cinthio's concern with the ruler's misuse of power as a civil crime with the moral play's concern with the misuse of power as a sin against God. 3. The Vice: Phallax, the evil counselor of *Promos and Cassandra,* is modeled after the Vice, the serio-comic heavy of the moral play who acts as an evil influence on the hero. In Cinthio's novella Juriste falls into sin of his own accord. In *Promos and Cassandra,* Phallax gives a shove. 4. Comic relief: Phallax's deputies, Gripax and Rapax, provide the roughhouse and bawdry that serve as comic relief in the sixteenth-century moral plays.

for grace. When he is pardoned by the King, we may infer that the King is acting as God's representative on earth, and that Promos has been forgiven in heaven as well as on earth.

Whetstone adds a subplot to the story that also deals with lechery. Lamia, a prostitute, achieves eminence in Julio by becoming the mistress of Phallax, Promos's deputy. When Promos repents and reforms, Lamia is publicly carted through the city.

Cinthio's *Epitia* and Whetstone's *Promos and Cassandra* differ markedly from the sources that Shakespeare had used for his earlier comedies. The sources of most of the Elizabethan comedies—*Rosalynde, Il Pecorone, Filesmena, Giletta of Narbona*—are stories of love and adventure in which the lovers overcome obstacles and finish in each other's arms. *Epitia* and *Promos and Cassandra* raise issues that are the stuff of serious drama. But, although Whetstone has a sound theme and a potentially dramatic story, he lacks the skill to achieve a successful play. Too much of the action of *Promos and Cassandra* occurs offstage and is related by the characters instead of being acted out; there is too much soliloquizing and explaining, too little dramatic confrontation. The main characters are little more than faceless speechifiers who deliver moralizing set pieces. Furthermore, the play is written for the most part in monotonously regular heptameter couplets (fourteeners), so that the serious speeches are badly compromised by their singsong rhythm. Shakespeare takes this imperfect play, and by applying a probing analysis of human behavior, grounded upon the best thinking of his day, as he does in his tragedies, he makes of it a powerful drama.

Measure for Measure follows *Promos and Cassandra* closely. Claudio gets his fiancée, Juliet, with child, and is sentenced to death for fornication. His sister, Isabella, pleads on his behalf to the deputy ruler, Angelo, who proposes the sexual ransom. Here Shakespeare makes a major change: Isabella does not submit to Angelo as Cassandra had to Promos. Angelo is tricked into thinking he has lain with Isabella, but he orders Claudio killed anyway. Claudio escapes execution. Angelo is brought to justice, repents, and is pardoned.

Shakespeare also adopts Whetstone's themes, expanding and developing them. To consider first the theme of the ruler's proper use of power, Shakespeare, like Whetstone, seeks to show that the highest form of temporal justice is that which imitates divine justice, and tempers strict administration of law with mercy. It is an underlying assumption of *Measure for Measure* that temporal power comes from God. This means that the ruler's authority may never be questioned by those who are ruled, but that the ruler must nevertheless remember that he is a frail man capable of error, and so must be careful in applying God's law to other men. This concern with the justice that one human being metes out to another is reflected in the title of the play, *Measure for Measure*. It is taken from Matthew 7:1-2, part of The Sermon on the Mount:

> Judge not, that ye be not judged.
> For with what judgement ye judge, ye shall
> be judged: and with what measure ye mete,
> it shall be measured to you again.

Christ is speaking to the multitudes—his humble followers —not to rulers, whose duty it is to judge; but the passage, when taken with the three verses that follow, obviously applies to rulers in general and to Angelo in particular.

And why beholdest thou the mote that is in thy brother's eye, but considerest not the beam that is in thine own eye?

Or how wilt thou say to thy brother, Let me pull the mote out of thine eye; and, behold, a beam is in thine own eye?

Thou hypocrite, first cast out the beam out of thine own eye; and then shalt thou see clearly to cast out the mote out of thy brother's eye.

In applying this text to rulers, Shakespeare interprets it as saying that he who would judge others must be free from sin himself; if he is not, he must not condemn others for a sin he shares. As the Duke says:

> He who the sword of heaven will bear
> Should be as holy as severe; . . .
> More nor less to others paying
> Than by self-offenses weighing.
>
> III, ii, 275, 276; 279, 280

Since, however, Christian doctrine teaches that man can never be entirely free from sin, nor can he be virtuous enough to earn salvation by his own merits, Shakespeare stresses that the temporal ruler should be very cautious in meting justice to his subjects. Unless they are definitely reprobates, he should show them the mercy that he hopes to receive when he himself is judged by God.

Angelo refuses to show Claudio any mercy. Angelo has never committed the sin of fornication, and is willing to be judged as he judges:

> When I, that censure him, do so offend,
> Let mine own judgement pattern out my death . . .
>
> II, i, 29–30

Angelo is dispensing absolute justice to Claudio—justice untempered by mercy. In fact, Shakespeare makes a point of having Escalus describe Angelo as Justice itself:

> My brother justice have I found so severe, that he
> hath forced me to tell him he is indeed Justice.
>   III, ii, 267–268

However, when Angelo becomes infatuated with Isabella,
his passions overwhelm his reason. He attempts to seduce
her, violating the strict standards of justice that he has
demanded of others. Although Angelo believes that he has
seduced Isabella, and so is guilty of fornication, this does
not deter him from ordering Claudio executed for the
same sin.

Just as Angelo champions justice but does not live up to
his ideal, so Isabella champions mercy but does not live
up to that ideal. In pleading with Angelo to spare Claudio,
Isabella admits that her brother is guilty, but she urges
Angelo to show him mercy. She tells Angelo:

> No ceremony that to great ones 'longs,
> Not the King's crown, nor the deputed sword,
> The marshal's truncheon, nor the judge's robe,
> Become them with one half so good a grace
> As mercy does.
>   II, ii, 59–63

She cites the sacrifice that Christ made to obtain mercy
for mankind:

> Why all the souls that were were forfeit once,
> And He that might the vantage best have took
> Found out the remedy.
>   II, ii, 73–75

She warns Angelo that he will some day be judged himself:

> How would you be
> If He, which is the top of judgement, should

But judge you as you are? O, think on that;
And mercy then will breathe within your lips,
Like man new made.

II, ii, 75–79

However, by offering to free her brother in return for her submission, Angelo forces Isabella to decide whether her brother shall live or die. In choosing to save her chastity and especially in her later treatment of Claudio, Isabella shows the same narrow legalism and lack of pity that Angelo does. When Isabella first asks Angelo to save Claudio, he refuses because the law demands Claudio's death. When Angelo asks Isabella to lie with him and so save Claudio, she refuses because the law of the church forbids fornication. Isabella fears that by committing fornication—regardless of the circumstances—she will risk eternal damnation. She argues that the "six or seven winters" of life that Claudio would gain by her sacrifice are not worth the price she would have to pay.

Better it were a brother died at once,
Than that a sister, by redeeming him,
Should die for ever.

II, iv, 106–8

Shakespeare obviously deviates from his sources in portraying his heroine's reaction to the sexual ransom proposition. Cinthio and Whetstone portray women who feel justified in committing fornication to save someone dear to them. Isabella, on the other hand, protests Christian righteousness in refusing to submit, and, paradoxically, falls into sin while trying to retain her virtue.

Whetstone considers Cassandra's decision to save her brother by submitting to Promos a moral act, a heroic sacrifice. He depicts Cassandra as a Christian martyr giving

up something she considers more sacred than life—her
honor—for the sake of someone she loves. So certain is
she of the innocence of her act that she asks God's blessing
as she leaves to meet Promos:

> But so or not, I must the venter give,
> No daunger feares the wight prickt foorth by neede:
> And thus lyke one more glad to dye than lyve,
> I forewarde set; God graunt me well to speede.
>   III, vii, 13–16

The King of Hungary, the arbiter of morality in *Promos and Cassandra,* treats the heroine as a virtuous and
wronged maiden, one who has made a heroic sacrifice and
deserves reward. This is the way Whetstone intends us to
see her.

Whetstone's opinion that Cassandra is virtuous and
heroic is justifiable according to Christian ethics. While
scriptural and ecclesiastical precepts underlie Christian
ethics, Christian moralists have always taken into account
the circumstances surrounding transgression. The law of
the church forbids fornication, for instance, but no less a
theologian than Augustine justifies fornication under certain circumstances. One he mentions is quite similar to
Isabella's situation.

In *De Sermone Domini in Monte Secundum Mattheaum,*
Augustine includes a sexual ransom tale.[12] A woman whose
husband will lose his life unless he raises a certain sum of
money can save him by submitting to a rich man who will
then pay the money. The woman holds that her husband
is the "conjugal master of her body to whom all her chastity (is) owed." He must decide whether or not she should
sell her favors for the ransom. The husband tells her that,

---

12. Bullough, *Sources,* 2: 418 ff.

since she will be doing the sexual act for his sake only, and there is no lust on her part, the act is not sinful. The woman submits, but the rich man reneges on his bargain. When she appeals to the governor of the city, he frees her husband and rewards her richly.

Augustine says of the case, "When the incident is told, man's moral sense is not so ready to condemn what happened in this woman's case at the behest of her husband, as we were shocked before when the case itself was being suggested without any illustration."[13]

Although Shakespeare might therefore have accepted Whetstone's view, he was apparently interested in a subtler and higher level of virtue. Unlike the heroines in Augustine, Cinthio, and Whetstone, Isabella not only refuses to save her brother but responds to his pleas with disgust and anger:

>   O you beast!
> O faithless coward! O dishonest wretch! . . .
> Heaven shield my mother play'd my father fair!
> For such a warped slip of wilderness
> Ne'er issued from his blood. Take my defiance!
> Die, perish! Might but my bending down
> Reprieve thee from thy fate, it should proceed.
> I'll pray a thousand prayers for thy death,
> No word to save thee.
>   III, i, 137–47

Perhaps if Isabella had refused Claudio in a gentle and pitying manner—more in sorrow than in anger—there might have been some question about how Shakespeare intends us to view her. However, it is clear from the immoderate, even wild, anger of her response, that Shakespeare regards her as sinful, not virtuous. Her taunt at the

---

13. *Ibid.,* p. 419.

hapless Claudio, questioning his legitimacy, and her threat to pray for his death, are signs not of righteous indignation, but of wrath, one of the seven deadly sins. Her treatment of her brother is clearly defective in human charity, and this defect requires remedying if she is to be truly virtuous.

Although Isabella and Angelo both sin, Shakespeare makes it clear that Angelo's sins are much blacker than Isabella's. Although Angelo does not accomplish the seduction of Isabella and the judicial murder of Claudio, his attempts to commit these acts are sinful, and so is his grave abuse of his power. Duke Vincentio has Isabella and Mariana accuse Angelo publicly, forcing him into a public repentance for his sins, with its attendant disgrace.

Although the Duke submits Isabella to the ordeal of mourning a brother who is still alive, he never makes her publicly recant her sins nor, for that matter, does he even charge her with them in private. Isabella's religious experience seems to be as much a fulfillment as a repentance; in forgiving Angelo she fulfills the Christian ideals of conduct that she has sought previously but never achieved.

Shakespeare makes his most important change in Whetstone's plot, the addition of the bed trick, in order to emphasize Isabella's religious fulfillment. It will be recalled in Whetstone's play that Cassandra's motive in pleading for the life of her seducer, Promos, is conjugal loyalty—he has become her husband. But Shakespeare's theme is not conjugal loyalty; it is the duty of the Christian to be merciful in judging a sinner. So, in *Measure for Measure,* Isabella does not plead for Angelo's life because she is his wife (the bed trick has assigned Mariana to that role); Isabella pleads for Angelo—her tormentor—because it is her Christian duty to put mercy above the strict observance of the law.

Isabella's decision to be merciful—her refusal to demand measure for measure (Angelo's death for Claudio's)—is the triumph of mercy over strict justice. Through Isabella's act Shakespeare stresses this theme, which he adopts from Whetstone. He drives home the point that the temporal ruler (and anyone else in the position of dealing out justice or mercy, like Isabella) should judge as he would be judged in heaven. He must remember Christ's warning: "With what measure ye mete, it shall be measured to you again." But Isabella's decision comes hard. She resists two pleas that she kneel. This final reluctance makes dramatically convincing an act that is not only a fulfillment of her earlier professions of sanctity but in fact a kind of repentance.

Shakespeare also treats another major theme from Whetstone and Cinthio, the sin of lechery. Like his predecessors, Shakespeare draws the distinction between fornication committed for love and fornication committed for lust. Escalus, a reliable narrator, describes Claudio's over-hasty bedding of his fiancée as a "fault." It is quite clear that Angelo's attempt to coerce Isabella to submit to him is a far more serious matter.

Like Whetstone, Shakespeare has a subplot that deals with lechery. He introduces a number of comic characters who trade in lust—Mistress Overdone, a bawd; Kate Keepdown, a whore; Pompey Bum, a pander; and Lucio, a dissolute young gentleman who is their chief customer. Here, as in many of the tragedies, the subplot treats a variation of the theme dealt with in the main plot.

But Shakespeare combines all his themes, mercy and justice, sin and repentance, love and lust, in his handling of Angelo. Angelo is guilty of three sins: the attempted seduction of Isabella, the attempted judicial murder of Claudio, and abuse of the powers of his office. According to Renaissance theology, an unsuccessful attempt—that is, the intention—to commit a forbidden act is sinful, though not as sinful as the commission of the act itself. So, although Angelo is frustrated in his attempt to seduce Isabella or to execute Claudio, the attempts themselves are sinful. As for Angelo's abuse of power, all temporal power derives ultimately from God, and any use of that power to achieve selfish and lawless ends is not only a civil wrong, but a sin.

Angelo's sins are followed by repentance. When Isabella and Mariana accuse him publicly of fornication and judicial murder, Angelo denies the charges. But when he discovers that the Duke knows that he is guilty, Angelo is stricken with remorse:

> O my dread lord,
> I should be guiltier than my guiltiness,
> To think I can be undiscernible,
> When I perceive your Grace, like power divine.
> Hath look'd upon my passes. Then, good Prince,
> No longer session hold upon my shame,
> But let my trial be mine own confession.
> Immediate sentence, then, and sequent death
> Is all the grace I beg.
>
> V, i, 371-79

Angelo's repentance is not a full one. The Homily describes four steps to repentance: contrition, confession, faith, and amendment of life. Angelo undergoes the first two. He is contrite—"earnestly sorry for his sins," as the Homily puts it. And he confesses to the Duke, God's representative on earth, that he has sinned. But the shock of being discovered has thrown Angelo into a state of despair. He lacks the faith that God, or the Duke, will deem him worthy of forgiveness. Speedy death is the only grace that Angelo begs. But Angelo's death wish is necessary to prove his genuine contrition on such short notice. Shakespeare considers the dramatic situation as well as the theological doctrine.

The Duke forgives Angelo anyway. As he brings Claudio forward, the Duke remarks:

> By this Lord Angelo perceives he's safe;
> Methinks I see a quick'ning in his eye.
> Well, Angelo, your evil quits you well
> V, i, 499–501

Angelo does not conquer his despair by faith that God's infinite mercy can save him, sinful as he is. His despair leaves him when he realizes that he has not really killed Claudio. Although Shakespeare treats sin and repentance far more seriously here than he did in *Two Gentlemen, Much Ado*, or *All's Well*, he still does not treat the theme successfully. Angelo sins only in intent. Although he tries to kill Claudio, he does not succeed. He repents a sin he has not really committed. And his repentance is only a partial one. Furthermore, it does not convince the audience as Isabella's does.

Shakespeare's failure to deal with sin and repentance altogether successfully in *Measure for Measure* is understandable in light of the source he is working with, and the tradition he is working in. In *Promos and Cassandra* Whetstone follows the traditions of Renaissance repentance comedy.

One of the main concerns of the writer of secular comedies of forgiveness is the avoidance of crime, for the crimes which are pardoned in these plays invariably turn out to have been committed only in intention. . . . The offenders in these plays are pardoned for crimes which they committed only within their

minds, but which they think they have committed in action. The
author of a secular comedy of forgiveness will either choose a
story in which the protagonist sins in intention only, or he will
modify the genuine sins of the narrative source so that they do
not take effect.[14]

The reason for this is that traditionally comedies deal with
follies rather than crimes, or with seeming crimes rather
than real ones.[15]

Another difficulty in treating a serious theme like sin
and repentance in comedy is that the conventions of comedy
are not really suited to it. *Measure for Measure,* for instance, retains a number of structural features from Shakespeare's earlier comedies, notably the complication comedy
conventions. Chief among these conventions is the use of
intrigue to resolve the plot. To keep Angelo from carrying
out his evil designs on Claudio and Isabella, Duke Vincentio
successfully pits "craft against vice" using, as we have
seen, a "bed trick" and a "head trick" to prevent Angelo
from doing any harm to his intended victims. Vincentio's
secretiveness, and his use of clever but unrealistic tricks, are
strongly reminiscent of the intriguing of Helena in *All's
Well.* (In opposing her craft to Bertram's vice, Helena
also uses the "bed trick.") The Duke's tricks also bear a
family resemblance to the ruses employed by Shylock and
Don John.

Intrigue works well in *The Two Gentlemen of Verona*
and *Much Ado about Nothing,* complication comedies with
a touch of melodrama that do not seriously examine an
important theme. In *Measure for Measure,* however, Duke
Vincentio's low-comedy tricks seem strangely out of keep-
ing with the high passion of Isabella's confrontations with

14. Hunter, p. 48.
15. *Ibid.,* p. 82.

Angelo and with her brother. The contrived nature of the
Duke's intrigue and the bawdy humor of the subplot dis-
tract attention from the serious theme.

Although Shakespeare retains the conventions of comedy
in *Measure for Measure,* he introduces an important feature from his tragedies. He replaces the one-dimensional
figures of his comedies with complex characters. In *Measure for Measure,* as in his tragedies, Shakespeare explores
his theme by making a thorough examination and ethical
evaluation of the mental processes of the central characters
as they struggle with moral decisions. Since I have already
discussed Isabella's character at some length, I will return
to Angelo's, in order to demonstrate that he closely resembles the protagonists of Shakespeare's tragedies.

Most critics traditionally have tended to think of Angelo
as a crafty, dissembling rogue who covers up his evil designs with a hypocritical show of virtue. W. W. Lawrence,
for instance, says that "it seems likely that Angelo is to be
regarded as having been a smooth rascal, who had been
successful in concealing his baseness."[16] Lawrence compares
Angelo to two of Shakespeare's dissembling villains, Iago
and Edmund. In making this comparison, however, Lawrence fails to take into account an important aspect of
Shakespeare's dramatic technique. Shakespeare's dissembling villains deceive the other characters, but always reveal
their true natures to the audience in asides or soliloquies.
Edmund and Iago make their evil intentions perfectly clear
to the audience. Angelo, on the other hand, tells us that he
has never been tempted to commit the sin of lechery until
he meets Isabella. We can be sure that Shakespeare intends
us to believe him. Angelo's own testimony is supported by
that of Isabella, who, in forgiving him, says,

---

16. *Shakespeare's Problem Comedies* (New York, 1931), p. 113.

> I partly think
> A due sincerity govern'd his deeds,
> Till he did look on me.
>
> V, i, 450–52

We may judge then that Angelo is not a villain like Edmund or Iago, thoroughly base and malicious, with no redeeming qualities. In fact, Angelo resembles the heroes of Shakespeare's tragedies far more closely than any character of his earlier comedies. He is a man who is basically noble, but who suffers from a defect in character, a wellnigh tragic flaw that causes him to commit the grievous error that brings his downfall.

First, he is mature, and he comports himself with severity and gravity. Certainly he is closer in age and demeanor to Macbeth, Othello, and Antony than he is to Proteus, Bertram, or Benedick. Second, he is a ruler like Antony, Macbeth, and Lear, not a private citizen like the comic heroes. Third, like the tragic heroes he is a man of great powers, a man preeminent in noble qualities. Duke Vincentio selects Angelo to rule Vienna primarily because he believes that Angelo's absolute probity and his strict ideas of discipline make him the ideal man to clean up the city's corruption. The Duke's opinion is shared by Escalus, who says:

> If any in Vienna be of worth
> To undergo such ample grace and honour
> It is Lord Angelo.
>
> I, i, 23–25

Finally, it is possible that like the tragic heroes, Angelo has a serious defect in his character, a tragic flaw. In a number of tragic heroes this defect takes the form of a besetting sin, one of the seven deadly sins. Lear, for instance, is afflicted with the sins of ire and pride; Coriolanus is given to pride; Antony is given to lechery. It is possible that Angelo's besetting sin is sloth, which in the Middle Ages and Renaissance involved spiritual narrowness as well as its modern connotation of laziness. Although this meaning of sloth was dying out in Shakespeare's day, we do know of at least one reference to it in his time, and it is possible that Shakespeare saw Angelo in these terms.

Sigfried Wenzel traces the origin of the Christian idea of sloth to the Egyptian monks who lived in the desert near Alexandria in the fourth century.[17] Sloth, or *accidia* (the medieval Latin term), was a demon who attacked the monk around noon, making him too sluggish to continue with his devotions. Through the eleventh century *accidia* meant primarily the physical phenomena of idleness and somnolence.[18] In the twelfth century, however, the scholastics began associating *accidia* with *tristitia,* sorrow. Aquinas, for instance, defines sloth as "an oppressive sorrow . . . a sluggishness of the mind which neglects to begin good."[19] To Aquinas *accidia* was the opposite of *gaudium* (joy), an aspect of the theological virtue *caritas* (charity).[20] Aquinas included among the daughters of sloth malice, spite, and despair.[21]

By Shakespeare's time the idea of sloth as spiritual narrowness had pretty well died out. Elizabethans normally understood the term to signify idleness. Spenser and Marlowe, for instance, both personify sloth as a sleepy, idle man. At least one reference to sloth as spiritual narrowness does persist in the seventeenth century, however. Shake-

---

17. *The Sin of Sloth* (Chapel Hill, 1960), p. 3.
18. Wenzel, p. 30.
19. *Summa Theologica*, Part II, Question 35, First Article.
20. Aquinas, Question 35.
21. Question 35, Fourth Article.

speare's fellow dramatist, Thomas Dekker, says in a pamphlet, *The Seven Deadly Sinnes of London* (1606):

> hee is not slothfull, that is onelye lazie, that onelye wastes his good houres, and his Siluer in Luxury, & licentious ease, or that onelye (like a standing water) does nothing, but gather corruption: no, hee is the true Slothfull man that does no good.[22]

Dekker lists as examples magistrates that leave their country in its hour of danger, physicians who desert the sick on their deathbed, and rulers who misappropriate public funds. Since Dekker is not a profoundly original thinker, it seems likely that he is referring to a tradition that still persisted.

Sloth as spiritual narrowness fits Angelo, whose dealings with Claudio show an utter lack of charity. Angelo manifests the traditional signs of the slothful man. Sloth traditionally afflicted monks and contemplatives.[23] While not in a cloister, Angelo is certainly monkish in his habits. He stifles the urge for the pleasure of the flesh by study and fast.

> . . . Lord Angelo, a man whose blood
> Is very snow-broth, one who never feels
> The wanton stings and motions of the sense,
> But doth rebate and blunt his natural edge
> With profits of the mind, study, and fast.
> I, iii, 57–61

According to the old tradition, Angelo's regimen is partially responsible for his slothful condition. Thirteenth-century divine Roger Bacon says,

> it is necessary for the mind's tranquillity that our human weakness sometimes turn away our mind from its attention to inner and outer cares and turn it toward comforts and recreations that

---

22. Ed. H. F. B. Brett-Smith (New York, 1922), p. 39.
23. Wenzel, p. 35.

are necessary for our body. Because otherwise our spirit becomes anxious, dull, *accidiosus,* sadder than it ought to be, weary with disgust of the good, querulous, and ready to frequent movements of impatience and anger. Therefore the greatest saints sometimes unbent from spiritual cares to comfort, and sometimes loosened their rigorous abstinence and shortened their excessive vigils.[24]

Angelo never unbent, and he became *accidiosus.*

Aquinas also points out that some forms of abstinence cause sloth:

if a man contemns the good things he has received from God, this, far from being a proof of humility, shows him to be ungrateful; and from suchlike contempt results sloth.[25]

Angelo certainly "contemns" the good things God sends mankind. Not only does he turn away from food and drink, he hardens his heart against the love of Mariana, spurning her when she loses her dowry.

In short, Angelo's self-denial is not virtuous; it is an unnatural turning away from the good things of God's creation. His refusal to partake of God's bounty is a sign of spiritual sickness, not health. Since Angelo's sloth manifests itself in abstinence rather than indulgence, Angelo appears to be a paragon of virtue. However, sloth steadily corrupts and weakens his will, so that when he is faced with a strong temptation—in the form of the beautiful Isabella—passion overpowers his will, and he sins.

Angelo moves from one sinful extreme, his heartless spurning of Mariana, to another, his lustful passion for Isabella. At the end of the play the Duke puts him on the correct path between these two extremes by marrying him to Mariana.

Measure for Measure deals with the sins against love—

---

24. Wenzel, p. 60.
25. Question 35, First Article.

premarital intercourse, dowry hunting, prostitution. The ending of the play celebrates the proper love relationship—marriage. Angelo marries Mariana. Isabella, who like Angelo has shunned life and love, apparently gives up the convent to marry the Duke. And Claudio, the lover whose sin sets off the whole train of events, finally gets to marry his fiancée, Juliet.

To summarize, *Measure for Measure* is different from Shakespeare's earlier repentance comedies. The others had used repentance as a plot device. *Measure for Measure* treats sin and repentance as a serious theme. In order to treat a serious theme in comedy, Shakespeare introduces a technique from his tragedies: he makes a thorough examination and ethical evaluation of the mental processes of the central characters as they struggle with moral decisions. But he does not treat convincingly their progress toward repentance, and Angelo, at least, leaves us unconvinced.

Because Shakespeare, following the tradition of repentance comedies, has Angelo sin only in intent and then repent hastily to wind up the play, *Measure for Measure* does not fully come to grips with the theme of sin and repentance. Shakespeare may well have realized the weakness of this splicing of intrigue comedy and a serious characterization of sinful humanity, yet, granted his Christian background, serious characterization would almost inevitably lead to a consideration of sin, and sin could have the happy ending appropriate to comedy only if it were followed by repentance. But a serious consideration of sin necessitated a serious treatment of repentance. At any rate, in his next repentance plays Shakespeare switched from comedy to another dramatic form better adapted to treat both sin and repentance fully, a variation of what today we call melodrama.

3

Pericles and *Cymbeline*
as Elizabethan Melodramas

AFTER *Measure for Measure,* Shakespeare did not treat the theme of sin and repentance again for five or six years. Then in 1609 or 1610 in *Cymbeline* and *The Winter's Tale* he returned to it. Now, however, he integrated it into the plays far more successfully than he had in *Measure for Measure. Cymbeline* and *The Winter's Tale* succeed in a convincing portrayal of repentance, whereas *Measure for Measure* fails, because they use a different dramatic form, one that contains strong elements of melodrama—sensational, bloody action, strong appeals to the emotions, and a happy ending. Although it has been customary to describe *Cymbeline* and *The Winter's Tale* as tragicomedies or romances, neither term adequately describes their form, and it is necessary to define that form before discussing its adequacy to a serious treatment of repentance. Before arguing for a new interpretation of *Cymbeline* and *The Winter's Tale* as melodramas, however, I must explain why I reject the traditional descriptions of the plays as tragicomedies or romances, since both terms have a long critical tradition behind them.

Tragicomedy was a term used in Jacobean England by Beaumont and Fletcher and others to describe plays in which heroes and heroines face grave dangers but escape safely in the end. Ashley Thorndike was the first critic to emphasize the similarities between Beaumont and Fletcher's tragicomedies and Shakespeare's last plays.[1] Thorndike argued that Shakespeare imitated Beaumont and Fletcher. But Thorndike overlooks a fundamental difference: in Shakespeare's melodramas, villains die bloody deaths, while in Beaumont and Fletcher's tragicomedies, no one dies.

Fletcher defines tragicomedy in his first experiment with the form, *The Faithful Shepherdess*. In an epistle to the reader he says:

> a tragi-comedy is not so called in respect of mirth and killing, but in respect it wants deaths, which is enough to make it no tragedy, yet brings some near it, which is enough to make it no comedy.[2]

Beaumont and Fletcher's best-known tragicomedies are *Philaster* and *A King and No King*. Both follow the formula in the epistle: they involve central characters in dangers too serious for comedy; yet extricate them, so that the plays are not tragedies either. The plays put royal protagonists of the sort common to Renaissance tragedy in familiar tragic situations. The main characters and central situation of *Philaster*, for instance, somewhat resemble those of *Hamlet*. Philaster, like Hamlet, is a prince wrongfully deprived of the throne by a usurper who deposes his father. The King of Sicily, like Claudius, would gladly kill or imprison the young prince, but is restricted by the Prince's popularity with the people. Philaster has other enemies as well: Pharamond, a Spanish prince who becomes Philaster's rival for the throne and for the King's daughter,

---

1. *The Influence of Beaumont and Fletcher upon Shakespeare* (New York, 1901).
2. Mermaid Edition (New York, 1949), ed. J. St. Loe Strachey, 2: 321.

Arethusa; and Megra, a corrupt lady in waiting who slanders Arethusa so effectively that Philaster is driven by jealousy to attack and gravely wound her. In the denouement, the usurper-King turns over the throne to Philaster, who wins Arethusa's forgiveness and her hand. In his last royal act the King sends Pharamond back to Spain, and pardons Megra, but banishes her from the court. So there is a relatively happy ending for the villains as well as for the hero and heroine, and the play is transformed at the last moment from a tragedy to a tragicomedy.

A King and No King is far lighter in tone than *Philaster,* thanks to a long farcical subplot. Yet Beaumont and Fletcher construct it along the same lines, bringing the protagonist to the brink of disaster, then extricating him. Arbaces, King of Iberia, harbors an incestuous love for his sister, Panthea. This has been fanned by a counselor, Gobrias, who, while Arbaces was away at war, wrote numerous "witching" letters extolling Panthea's beauties and her love for Arbaces. Arbaces struggles vainly against the passion, and finally is about to murder Gobrias for involving him in it when Gobrias reveals that Arbaces is neither the rightful king of Iberia nor Panthea's brother. Indeed, he is Gobrias's own son, who had been substituted as a changeling to give the old impotent king of Iberia an heir. Arbaces, no king, steps down from the throne and marries Panthea.

Philaster and *A King,* with their happy ending for all, are fundamentally different from melodrama, which provides a happy ending for sympathetic characters but usually kills off the villains. The merciful treatment of the King, Pharamond, and Megra in *Philaster* contrasts sharply with the fate Shakespeare accords to Antiochus and his daughter, Cleon and Dionyza, and Cloten and the

Queen, the villains of *Pericles* and *Cymbeline*. In short, tragicomedy abruptly reverses an action apparently moving toward catastrophe, and allows everyone to participate in the happy ending. Melodrama provides a double ending, a happy fate for the sympathetic characters, and a bloody one for the villains.

The term "romance," used almost universally today by critics to describe Shakespeare's last plays, is also a poor descriptive term. It is vague to the point of meaninglessness. As Stanley Wells puts it:

> The very word is shadowy, having associations with literature of various kinds, forms, and periods; with modes of sensibility; with languages; and with love. It can be spoken with an auspicious or a dropping eye; with a sob, a sigh, or a sneer; with the aspiration to define or with a defiance of definition. It means so much that often it means nothing at all.[3]

Shakespeare himself never used the word. It was used in the Renaissance, but never to describe dramas. The NED supplies these definitions:

> A tale in verse embodying the adventures of some hero of chivalry . . . and belonging in matter and form to the ages of knighthood . . .

and

> a fictitious narrative in prose of which the scene and incidents are very remote from those of ordinary life.

As these indicate, the term romance was used in the Renaissance to describe a type of subject matter, the adventures of a hero of chivalry, and the treatment which the subject

---

3. "Shakespeare and Romance," *Later Shakespeare,* Stratford-Upon-Avon Studies 8 (London, 1966), p. 49.

is accorded: the scenes and incidents are glamorized and idealized, made remote from those of ordinary life. There is no prescribed tone or ending. Romances could end tragically, with the death of the hero, as does Malory's *Morte d'Arthur,* or happily with the triumph of the protagonists, as Sidney's *Arcadia* does.

So although *Pericles, Cymbeline,* and *The Winter's Tale* are undeniably romantic in subject and treatment—as are many of Shakespeare's earlier plays—the term "romance" does not describe them adequately, since it tells us nothing about the form of the play. If we are to use the term "romance" to describe the last plays, it would be better to use the adjectival form "romantic," and couple it with a term designating the genre. This is in line with traditional description of Shakespeare's earlier plays. *As You Like It, Twelfth Night,* and *Much Ado about Nothing* are traditionally called "romantic comedies." No term exactly fits Shakespeare's last plays, but the one that comes the closest is "romantic melodrama."

"Melodrama," the NED tells us, was first used in the nineteenth century to describe plays in which the action was accompanied by orchestral music "appropriate to the situation. Now," the definition continues, "the name denotes a dramatic piece characterized by sensational incident and violent appeals to the emotions, but with a happy ending."

Today melodrama survives chiefly in the cinema, in the form of the "cops and robbers" movie, the spy film, and the "western." These are characterized by violent action—gun fights, bombings, high-speed chases. They appeal to the emotions of the audience by pitting against each other stereotyped characters who represent, on the simplest level, the forces of good and evil. There are idealized heroes

with whom the audience sympathizes and identifies—
strong, silent cowboys and detectives, sophisticated secret
agents, all loved by beautiful heroines. Their evil oppo-
nents—outlaws, Indians, gangsters, and Communist spies—
are portrayed in the same bald terms. In the early stages
of the movie the villain prevails. The audience responds
with pity and concern for the hero, and with hatred for his
enemy. There is always a peripeteia, however, and the hero
triumphs and wins the girl. The villain dies a violent death.

The Elizabethans wrote plays very similar in pattern to
these films. The knight was the prototype of the lawman
or secret agent of today's melodrama. Like his twentieth-
century counterparts, the knight battles villains and infidels,
and triumphs in the end.

Only a handful of these plays survive, but there is evidence that they were once quite popular.[4] Among those
that have survived are Robert Greene's *Alphonsus of Arragon,* Thomas Heywood's *The Four Prentices of London,*
and the anonymous *Sir Clyomon and Sir Clamydes* and
The Trial of Chivalry.

The earliest of these plays is *Sir Clyomon and Sir Clamydes* (*c.* 1570). As in modern melodrama, the characters
of this play are stereotypes. The protagonists, Sir Clyomon,
The Knight of the Golden Shield, and Sir Clamydes, The
White Knight, are faceless, idealized, chivalric heroes. The

---

4. In addition to the plays I discuss, Alfred Harbage's *Annals of
English Drama* lists the following titles of lost plays: *The Red Knight,
The Irish Knight, The Solitary Knight, Herpetulus the Blue Knight and
Perobia,* and *The Knight in the Burning Rock.* Although of course we
cannot be certain of the nature of these plays, their titles suggest that
they are melodramas of adventure like *Sir Clyomon and Sir Clamydes.*
Furthermore, two parodies of adventure melodrama survive, Peele's *Old
Wives' Tale* and Beaumont's *The Knight of the Burning Pestle.* Since
satirists usually lampoon only popular works, I think we are safe in
assuming that melodramas of knightly adventure were popular in Elizabethan England.

heroines, Neronis, Princess of the Isle of Strange Marshes, and Juliana, Princess of Denmark, are beautiful and virtuous, but they lack individual identity. So do the villains, Thrasellus, the heavy, and Brian Sans Foy, a comic figure. Initially the villains oppress the sympathetic characters. Brian Sans Foy casts a spell on Sir Clamydes, and Thrasellus abducts Neronis. Ultimately, the play ends happily for the heroes and heroines: Clyomon kills Thrasellus, and Clamydes puts Brian Sans Foy to flight. The curtain descends as heroes and heroines plan their weddings.

The next Renaissance melodrama is Greene's *Alphonsus of Arragon* (*c.* 1587), a play far darker in tone than *Sir Clymon,* and much closer in spirit to modern melodramas. Alphonsus, a model, warlike knight, is denied accession to the throne because his father, the king of Arragon, is wrongfully deposed. Alphonsus vows to win back his father's kingdom, and does so by slaughtering the usurper and his evil allies. He decorates his tent with the heads of his enemies, sparing only Amurack, the great Turk, for the sake of his daughter, whom Alphonsus marries.

The two final plays, Thomas Heywood's *The Four Prentices of London* (1600), and the anonymous *The Trial of Chivalry* (*c.* 1601), do not have central characters. Instead, a group of sympathetic characters, all equally heroic and faceless, oppose a group of faceless, malevolent antagonists. As usual in melodrama, good prevails over evil and the stage is littered with dead villains.

In short, the four works are melodramas in the modern sense of the word. They are plays of violent action that make a strong appeal to the emotions of the audience, and end happily for the heroes and bloodily for the villains.

Shakespeare first experimented with melodrama in *Pericles* (1607 or 1608). The play is clearly inferior to his

other works. Indeed, scholars believe that he was not the
sole author but merely a collaborator.[5] Yet, although the
play is poor, and although it has no serious theme itself,
Shakespeare evidently saw that its form might, with some
changes, provide a better medium than comedy for dealing
with the theme of sin and repentance.

Pericles has much in common with Elizabethan melodramas. The play opens on a melodramatic note. Pericles
comes to the court of King Antiochus to woo the King's
daughter. This is a courtship common to fairy tale, in
which the suitor must solve a riddle in order to win the
lady. Since the answer to the riddle is that the king is living
incestuously with his daughter, an accurate guess is just as
hazardous as an inaccurate one; the penalty for both is
death. Prior suitors have guessed wrong, and their heads,
hanging on the walls, serve as a gruesome warning to Pericles. Shakespeare had used the marriage guessing game
before in *The Merchant of Venice,* but there the penalty
for guessing wrong was taking a vow of celibacy. This is
nothing trivial, of course, but it is still appropriate to comedy. But in *Pericles* the decaying heads on the walls are the
stuff of melodrama.

Pericles, who sees through the riddle, realizes that his
only course is flight. He is shipwrecked on the shores of
Pentapolis, where the king, Simonides, has ordained a
tournament for his daughter's hand. Although weakened by
his ordeal at sea, and poorly armed, Pericles nevertheless
wins the tournament and the lady. In this he typifies the
prowess of the melodramatic hero—traditionally not only
a paragon of virtue, but invincible in combat.

Pericles marries Thaisa and later sets out for Tyre with

5. *Pericles,* ed. F. D. Hoeniger (Cambridge, Mass.: The Arden Shakespeare, 1963), pp. lii ff.

his wife, who is now pregnant. During a storm, Thaisa
apparently dies while delivering a daughter, Marina, and
is set adrift in a casket. Pericles leaves Marina at the
neighboring kingdom of Tarsus, whose king and queen,
Cleon and Dionyza, he had once befriended. He does not
intend to see her again until she marries.

Cleon and Dionyza raise the girl until she is fourteen,
when the Queen, envious that Marina is more beautiful
than her own daughter, decides to kill her. The assassin,
one Leonine, takes Marina to the seashore, but just as he
is about to kill her, pirates come and carry her off. The
pirates sell her into a brothel in Mytilene. However, Marina's purity is of such power that it cools her eager clients,
including Lysimachus, the governor of Mytilene. They not
only leave her unsullied, but abandon their lechery. Finally,
Pericles discovers and rescues Marina. Then some magic
music is heard, and Pericles is charmed into a sleep. The
goddess Diana appears in a dream and tells Pericles where
to find his long-lost wife, and the family is reunited. Lysimachus and Marina are then betrothed, and the play ends
happily for everyone except the villains. We are told that
the people of Tarsus tear Cleon and Dionyza limb from
limb.

As we can see, from the opening spectacle of the throne
room with its severed heads to Cleon and Dionyza's violent end, *Pericles* is melodrama. Clearly it is no tragedy.
The happy ending for Pericles and his family precludes
this. Just as clearly, the play is not a comedy; the villains
die. Most anthologies of Shakespeare's plays group *Pericles* with the comedies, but it is obvious from the opening
scene that the play is not comic. The perilous guessing game
strikes a note too sinister for comedy.

Pericles is filled throughout with the sensational inci-

dents common to melodrama: Pericles' flight and shipwreck; Thaisa's apparent death and resurrection; Marina's
imprisonment in a brothel.

Furthermore, the play employs the usual melodramatic
appeals to the emotions. The audience trembles for Marina
when an assassin tries to murder her, and suffers with her
in the brothel. The audience fears for Pericles when he
flees from Antiochus, and pities him when he despairs over
the death of Marina. And they hate Antiochus and
Dionyza.

Finally, the characters are the stereotypes of melodrama.
Pericles is an all-wise ruler and peerless warrior, but hardly
distinguishable from other melodramatic heroes. F. D. Hoeniger, the Arden editor, describes him as "an impeccably
good man, a man without defect."[6] This judgment may be
too favorable, but it suggests the tone of the play.

Both Thaisa and Marina are, of course, virtuous and
beautiful, but totally faceless. Neither possesses a single
discernible fault. This perfection differentiates them from
the heroines of Shakespeare's comedies, who are indubita-
bly attractive, but possess normal human frailties. Antiochus and Dionyza are stage villains.

The people of *Pericles,* wooden characters of melodrama, seldom have convincing motives for their actions.
For instance, when Cerimon brings Thaisa back to life, we
might logically expect her to take the first boat for Tyre
to join her husband and child. Instead, she enters a convent. Pericles' handing over his daughter, whom he loves,
to foster parents is equally puzzling.

Pericles, then, is a melodrama, in the tradition of Elizabethan melodramas. It differs from Shakespeare's earlier
plays, all of which, save for the chronicle plays and *Troilus*

and Cressida, were either clearly comedies or tragedies.[7]

While the evidence is conclusive that *Pericles* is a melodrama, a form that Shakespeare had not used before, the
fact remains that it closely follows its sources, Gower's
tale of Apollonius of Tyre, from *Confessio Amantis,* and
Lawrence Twine's *Pattern of Painful Adventures.* These
tales end happily for the sympathetic characters and bloodily for the villains. It may be contended, then, that Shakespeare is not experimenting with a new form, but simply
following his source. The evidence does not support this.
Shakespeare had dealt with tales like Gower's and Twine's
before, changing details in their plots to suit his purpose.
For example, *As You Like It* is based on Lodge's *Rosalynde,* a tale which also ends happily for the sympathetic
characters and bloodily for the villain. But here Shakespeare alters the story, changing the death of the usurping
Duke to a religious conversion in order to keep *As You
Like It* comic. Had the Duke died a bloody death, and had
the incident been properly emphasized, the play would have
moved into the realm of melodrama.

In *Pericles,* on the other hand, Shakespeare leaves the
story as he finds it. He could easily have made some minor
changes and spared the villains. Had he done this, and had
he lightened the tone by cutting down the bathos and by
interjecting more humor, the play would have been a comedy. That he did neither is significant. Never before had he
written a melodrama; in *Pericles* he does. In his next plays,
Cymbeline and *The Winter's Tale,* he continues to use elements of melodrama, although he transforms them into a
new kind of drama. It seems clear, then, that in *Pericles*
he was experimenting with a dramatic form that was new

---

7. Several of Shakespeare's earlier comedies have melodramatic scenes
(the trial scene in *The Merchant of Venice;* jilting of Hero in *Much
Ado*) but the plays, taken as wholes, are comedies.

to him, but for which he had ample precedent on the
Elizabethan stage.

Pericles paves the way for *Cymbeline* and *The Winter's
Tale*. As Geoffrey Bullough says, *Pericles* was a "labora-
tory for experiments he was to apply more fruitfully in the
last years of his career."[8]

Cymbeline returns to the sin-repentance pattern of moral
choice broached in *Measure for Measure*. This time, however, Shakespeare is more successful in dramatizing the
theme, because he abandons the form of complication comedy and uses instead the elements of melodrama that he
had experimented with in *Pericles*. The conventions of
melodrama are better suited than those of comedy for
dealing with serious action and a serious theme. However,
melodrama does not traditionally have complex, psychologically realistic characters, and yet this sort of protagonist is needed for a play that deals with the sin-repentance
pattern of moral choice. In creating such a protagonist in
Posthumus, Shakespeare departs from melodrama as it
had been traditionally written. He makes the first step
toward creating a new form of drama, one that combines
serious, bloody action with a happy ending, but that does
away with stereotyped characters, and internalizes the
struggle between good and evil within the souls of the
characters themselves. He completes the transition to the
new form in his next play, *The Winter's Tale*. *Cymbeline*
may be seen as a way station: it looks back to *Pericles*, a
melodrama of the traditional Elizabethan sort, and forward to *The Winter's Tale*, the new form of drama.

Cymbeline retains many of the elements of melodrama

---

8. *Narrative and Dramatic Sources of Shakespeare* (New York, 1966)
6: 374. In a future study I plan to investigate whether *Henry IV*, parts
one and two, and *Henry V* are not also melodramas.

that Shakespeare used in *Pericles*. All of the characters save Posthumus are stereotypes. The action is sensational, and it ends happily for the sympathetic characters, bloodily for most of the villains. The plot is constructed on the familiar melodramatic pattern of beauty and the beast(s). In terms of the action of the play (though not of the theme) Imogen, the beauty, is the central character.[9] She is surrounded by lecherous, murderous villains who conspire to ravish and kill her. And Imogen has to contend not only with the villains, but also with the hero, her husband, Posthumus. Tricked by one of the villains, he too becomes a monster and attempts to murder her.

Imogen is a typical heroine of melodrama in that she is less a realistic character than a type or a symbol. She is the idealized, ethereal princess of fairy tale or romance, the symbol of female virtue and chastity.[10] If she seems more lifelike than most cardboard heroines of melodrama, it is because Shakespeare gives her some brilliant and moving lines, particularly in the scene in which Pisanio shows her the letter in which Posthumus orders her death. But no matter how much we are taken with her, we must realize that she is in no way psychologically complex or realistic.

Her actions illustrate her unreal nature. For instance, when she learns that her husband plans to kill her, she disguises herself as a boy, and sets out on an arduous journey, on foot, hoping eventually to join him. Even if her loyalty to her murderous husband is understandable in terms of realistic human behavior, her transvestite odyssey is, of course, simply the stuff of fairy tale.

---

9. Cymbeline, for whom the play is named, is a relatively minor character in terms of both the plot and theme. The play is named after him probably because he is the highest ranking character in it. In this respect it is similar to *Julius Caesar*.

10. See J. M. Nosworthy's introduction to the Arden *Cymbeline* (London, 1955), p. lx.

Imogen's oppressors are also types traditional to melo-drama. Iachimo is the heavy, a stage villain who has no discernible motives for his malicious behavior. Italian villains were common in Elizabethan drama because of English ideas about the Italian character, traceable in part to xenophobia and in part to a misunderstanding of Machiavelli.[11] To the Elizabethans a villain from "drug-damned Italy," as Imogen calls it, conjured up much the same response as a member of the Mafia does to a modern American audience. It is interesting to note that Iachimo is the only character in the play referred to as Italian. Other characters from Italy are called Romans. Irrational as it may sound, *Rome* had far better connotations for the English than *Italy*.

In the familiar melodramatic confrontation between good and evil the despicable Iachimo schemes to seduce the angelic Imogen, who, of course, is completely unaware of her danger. The scene in which he prowls her boudoir, notes a mole beneath one of her breasts, and steals a bracelet from her arm is melodrama at its most melodramatic. Imogen, beautiful and innocent, lies asleep, while a despicable villain skulks around her room, leering at her as she lies half naked, gathering the information that will compromise her honor and possibly endanger her life.

The scene in which Iachimo convinces Posthumus that he has seduced Imogen is equally melodramatic. Although Iachimo bluntly tells Posthumus that he has lain with Imogen, Posthumus is slow in believing it, and the tension mounts steadily as Iachimo describes the bedroom and shows the bracelet. The climax comes when Iachimo describes the mole, and says,

---

11. See Fredson Bowers, *Elizabethan Revenge Tragedy* (Princeton, 1940), pp. 47 ff.

By my life,
I kiss'd it; and it gave me present hunger
To feed again, though full.

II, iv, 136–38

Posthumus storms out in a rage, threatening to tear his wife "limb meal."

The atmosphere of the scene is poisonous. What A. C. Bradley says about *Othello* applies here as well: "There is no subject more exciting than sexual jealousy rising to the pitch of passion."[12] As Posthumus becomes convinced that Imogen has cuckolded him, the stage crackles with hate.

Another of Imogen's bestial enemies is Cloten, her stepbrother, who wants to supplant Posthumus as her husband. Cloten is less dangerous than Iachimo, but only because he is stupid. He is so much a fool that he is, at least in part, a comic figure. Granville-Barker describes him as "a comic character drawn with a savagely serious pen."[13] But there is a sinister side to Cloten, too. He may be as stupid as Dogberry, but he is also as malevolent as John the Bastard. He is lecherous, vengeful, and violent. He is most formidable and dangerous when he sets out in pursuit of Imogen. Imogen tells Cloten that Posthumus's "meanest garment" is dearer to her than he, Cloten, is. He procures a suit belonging to Posthumus and declares:

With that suit upon my back will I ravish her,—first kill him, and in her eyes; there shall she see my valour, which will then be a torment to her contempt,—he on the ground, my speech of insultment ended on his dead body; and when my lust hath dined,— which, as I say, to vex her I will execute in the clothes that she

---

12. *Shakespearean Tragedy* (New York: Meridian Books, 1955), p. 146.
13. *Prefaces to Shakespeare: Second Series* (London, 1930), p. 304.

so praised,—to the court I'll knock her back, foot her home again.
                                                        III, v, 141–49

The speech is pure melodrama. The villain threatens to kill her husband, ravish the heroine, and then kick her home.

But melodrama operates by the rules of poetic justice, and Cloten never gets to carry out his violent plan. Instead he suffers a bloody death, the traditional fate of the villain of melodrama. Guiderius, a long-lost son of Cymbeline, meets Cloten in a forest in Wales, fights with him, and cuts off his head. The fight takes place off-stage, but Guiderius comes in immediately afterwards waving Cloten's bloody head. The effect is far more striking and melodramatic than anything in *Pericles,* and certainly far too bloody for comedy.

The last of the beasts is the Queen, Imogen's step-mother. She is the stereotyped evil stepmother of fairy tale. Her relationship to Imogen is the same as that of the Queen to Snow White in the Grimms' tale, and her character is the same as the Grimms' Queen. And like the Queen in "Snow White," Cymbeline's Queen poisons her daughter, fortunately not fatally. She is, in short, to use Nosworthy's phrase, "a malign puppet," "the embodiment of malevolence."[14]

Although the Queen dies in bed, she expires in a paroxysm of hate, and in a sense her death fits the normal pattern of violent deaths traditional for the villains of melodrama. Before she dies she gives what might be termed a "black confession," repenting that she had not been able to do more evil while she was alive. She had planned not only to poison Imogen, but to give the King a "mortal

---

14. *Cymbeline,* p. lxv.

mineral" that would have killed him "by inches." This
anti-confession is an obvious contrast to Posthumus's Christian repentance.

Imogen and the villains are the white and black characters typical of melodrama. But *Cymbeline* parts from
traditional melodrama in its portrayal of the hero. Although Posthumus is introduced to us as the stereotyped,
idealized melodramatic hero, he soon changes. He makes
two crucial moral choices—to sin and to repent—and so
undergoes a process of degeneration and regeneration. As
he does in tragedies, Shakespeare makes the acts of choice
an important part of the play, and he works them out in
detail according to Elizabethan psychological theory.[15] Although it is true that Posthumus hardly resembles the
heroes of the tragedies—he seems dwarfed in comparison
with Macbeth, Othello, or Antony—yet like these heroes
he is the focus of a study of the destructive effects of sin
on the human psyche. The tragic heroes, of course, are
destroyed by their sins. Posthumus, like Angelo in *Measure
for Measure,* repents and is redeemed.

As the play opens, Posthumus is presented to us as the
impossibly virtuous and accomplished hero of melodrama.
In the opening scene of the play the first Lord describes
him as

> a creature such
> As, to seek through the regions of the earth
> For one his like, there would be something failing
> In him that should compare. I do not think
> So fair an outward and such stuff within
> Endows a man but he.
>   I, i, 19–24

---

15. Cf. Virgil K. Whitaker, *Shakespeare's Use of Learning* (San Marino,
1964), p. 246.

However, Posthumus's actions soon prove him less perfect, if more human, than his description. He makes the ill-fated wager with Iachimo, as we have seen, and he attempts to kill Imogen. Although his attempt to kill Imogen is clearly sinful, whether or not the wager itself was wrong is a vexed question.

Although by modern standards Posthumus's behavior in making the wager may seem despicable, or even immoral, it is possible that the Elizabethans thought it justifiable. W. W. Lawrence argues this point. According to his interpretation Posthumus shows "the confidence of a trusting husband, willing to go to any extreme to show his confidence in his wife's integrity."[16] Iachimo proposes the bet to Posthumus in the form of a challenge, and Lawrence contends that Elizabethan ideals of knightly behavior decreed that it was the "solemn duty of a knight not to hesitate when the virtues and excellence of his lady are called in question."[17] In refusing the wager Posthumus would have reflected discredit on the honor of both of them.

It should be pointed out, however, that often in other plays Shakespeare makes it clear that honor is merely a euphemism for pride, the deadliest of the seven deadly sins. For instance, Othello describes himself as an "honourable murderer," Romeo fights and kills Tybalt partially to clear his "stain'd reputation," Hotspur allows his quest for honor to lead him into a lawless and disastrous rebellion, and Cassius works on Brutus's sense of honor in convincing him that he should take part in the assassination of Caesar. In *Cymbeline*, however, there are no clear guideposts to tell us how we are to react to the wager. Pisanio tries to stop the bet from being made, and his disapproval

---

16. *Shakespeare's Problem Comedies* (New York, 1931), p. 189.
17. *Ibid.,* p. 189.

would seem to be an indictment of Posthumus. But, on the other hand, when Iachimo repents he defends Posthumus's motives in taking the bet:

> He, true knight,
> No lesser of her honour confident
> Than I did truly find her, stakes this ring;
> And would so, had it been a carbuncle
> Of Phoebus' wheel, and might so safely, had it
> Been all the worth of's car.
>
> V, v , 186–91

Clearly Shakespeare intends us to believe here that Iachimo has reformed, and that his testimony about Posthumus is reliable. In sum, then, it seems probable that Shakespeare intends us to believe Posthumus justified in making the wager.

There is no doubt, of course, that Posthumus sins in trying to kill his wife. That a man is morally wrong to order his wife's murder may seem to need no arguing, but I will briefly discuss Posthumus's way of thinking in order to show how Shakespeare depicts it in accordance with Elizabethan psychological theory.

First of all, in defense of Posthumus it may be said that the evidence Iachimo gives him of Imogen's infidelity is strong, and consequently his anger at her is certainly understandable. However, Posthumus is wrong, sinfully wrong, to let his anger so overcome his reason that he attempts to murder Imogen. Even if she had betrayed him, Posthumus would have been wrong to attempt to take her life. Both civil law and Christian teaching forbid a man from taking the law into his own hands. However, the case is even stronger against Posthumus in light of the fact that Imogen did not betray him. He owed it to himself as

well as to her to look further into the matter—to ask
her for her side of the story, for instance. Christian doctrine is clear on this point as well. Like Claudio, Posthumus
believes, to use Hooker's words, the "show of that which
is not," partially because of the "inveigling" of that devil
incarnate, Iachimo, and partially because his will, influenced
by his passions, overrules his reason.[18]

It is clear that Posthumus's anger is not simply righteous
indignation. His violence and incoherence show that anger
has completely subdued his reason:

> O, that I had her here, to tear her limb meal!
> I will go there and do't, i' the court, before
> Her father. I'll do something—
>
> II, iv, 147–49

His friend, Philario, recognizes the danger of his mood,
and although his words

> Quite besides
> The government of patience!
> II, iv, 149–50

sound like an understatement to modern ears, he is fully
aware that there is a danger that Posthumus will do something violent.

Philario's fears are justified. After delivering a mi-
sogynistic tirade worthy of Timon, Posthumus writes to
his servant Pisanio ordering him to kill Imogen. Pisanio
will not carry out the order, but since he is afraid of
overtly disobeying his master, he sends him a blood-stained
handkerchief as proof that he has killed Imogen.

Posthumus is a basically good man, and when his anger

---

18. See above, p. 17.

cools, he is horrified at what he has asked Pisanio to do. Altough he still believes Imogen to be guilty, he repents that, as he thinks, he has had her killed.

In its broad outlines Posthumus's repentance follows the four steps described in the Homily "Of Repentance." Many critics who recognize that Posthumus undergoes repentance fail to understand fully how he acts because they get their ideas about repentance from Luther, Aquinas, and other theologians, rather than from "Of Repentance."[19] The Homily has much in common with these theologians, of course, but in certain key points it differs, and this difference is important to understanding Posthumus's behavior.

The fact that *Cymbeline* is set in pre-Christian Britain has no bearing on Posthumus's repentance. Anachronisms seldom bother Shakespeare. His characters, whatever the period and country, generally think and act like Elizabethan Englishmen.[20] The language that Posthumus uses makes it absolutely clear that he is undergoing a Christian repentance. There is some question, however, about the identity of Jupiter, the god who appears and influences Posthumus's repentance. I will discuss this below.

In the first scene in which we see Posthumus after his attempt to murder his wife, he has landed in England as a member of the invasion party from Rome. The Romans are attacking England to collect the tribute that Cymbeline has withheld from them. Posthumus has been impressed into the Roman army. He is clutching the blood-stained handkerchief from Pisanio. His soliloquy shows his disgust and sorrow at what he has done.

---

19. Cf. Nosworthy's note to the "welcome bondage" soliloquy, *Cymbeline,* p. 162, and R. G. Hunter's chapter on *Cymbeline* in *Shakespeare and the Comedy of Forgiveness* (New York, 1965).
20. See Bradley, p. 153.

> Yea, bloody cloth, I'll keep thee, for I wish'd
> Thou shouldst be colour'd thus. You married ones,
> If each of you should take this course, how many
> Must murder wives much better than themselves
> For wrying but a little!
>
> V, i, 1–5

Posthumus is undergoing what the Homily calls contrition, the "thorough feeling of our sins," which is the first step of repentance.

Posthumus's contrition is clearly genuine, because although he still believes Imogen to be guilty, he forgives her. Traditionally forgiveness is a part of repentance. R. G. Hunter cites Luther and English theologian Alexander Nowell to prove this point,[21] but a more familiar instance, and one that Shakespeare and the Elizabethans were more likely to know, is that of the Lord's Prayer:

> forgive us our trespasses, as we forgive those who trespass against us.

Despite the fact that his sorrow is genuine, Posthumus has only begun his contrition. He is still unable to take the full responsibility for his act. He berates his servant Pisanio for following his orders, and he questions the justice of the gods for permitting him to commit his crime.

> O Pisanio!
> Every good servant does not all commands;
> No bond but to do just ones, Gods! if you
> Should have ta'en vengeance on my faults, I never
> Had liv'd to put on this; so had you sav'd
> The noble Imogen to repent, and struck
> Me, wretch, more worth your vengeance.
>
> I, i, 5–11

---

21. *Forgiveness*, p. 159.

Until Posthumus is able fully to accept his guilt, he cannot proceed to the next stages of repentance—confession, faith, and amendment of life. He prays to the gods to help accomplish these steps.

> do your best wills,
> And make me blest to obey!

> Gods, put the strength o' th' Leonati in me!
> To shame the guise o' th' world, I will begin
> The fashion: less without and more within.
> V, i, 16–17, 31–33

Posthumus disguises himself as a British peasant, and after fighting valiantly with the British against the Roman army with which he came, he tells the British that he is a Roman soldier, and surrenders to them. They imprison him.

In prison he speaks a soliloquy showing that he has progressed further towards repentance:

> Most welcome, bondage! for thou art a way,
> I think, to liberty . . .
>   . . . My conscience, thou art fetter'd
> More than my shanks and wrists. You good gods, give me
> The penitent instrument to pick that bolt;
> Then free for ever! Is't enough I am sorry?
> So children temporal fathers do appease;
> Gods are more full of mercy. Must I repent,
> I cannot do it better than in gyves,
> Desir'd more than constrain'd . . .
> V, iv, 3–19

Posthumus now fully accepts the responsibility for his guilt, confesses it to the gods, and is eager to repent his sin. However, he lacks the thing most necessary for repentance, faith that he will be saved. In hating himself for his first sin, he commits the sin of despair. The repentance he seeks, one filled with punishment and ending with death, is what the Homily describes as "Cain's or Judas' repentance." According to the Homily, Judas was "sorrowful and heavy, yea, . . . filled with anxiety and vexed of mind for that which he had done." Furthermore, Judas openly confessed what he had done, though it was a dangerous thing to do. And he made a "certain kind of satisfaction" when he threw back the money he had taken. Yet, says the Homily, he was "cast away" because he "wanted faith, whereby he did despair of the goodness and mercy of God."[22]

Posthumus's state of mind is comparable to that of Judas. His shame and despair drive him to long for punishment and death. When he prays for the "penitent instrument" to free his conscience, he means that he wants to atone for his sin by penance—self-abasement and mortification. While the Catholics held penance a necessary part of repentance, the Homily, with its Protestant emphasis on faith rather than works, says:

> This was commonly the penance that Christ enjoined sinners, Go thy way and sin no more. Which penance we shall never be able to fulfil, without the special grace of him that doth say, Without me ye can do nothing.

> p. 544

Posthumus's despair makes him long for death. He hopes that by dying he can "make satisfaction" for his sin.

>   to satisfy,
>   If of my freedom 'tis the main part, take

---

22. "Of Repentance," *Certain Sermons or Homilies Appointed to be Read in the Time of Queen Elizabeth of Famous Memory* (Oxford, 1844), p. 543.

No stricter render of me than my all. . . .
For Imogen's dear life take mine . . .
                                        V, iv, 16–22

Satisfaction is a technical term. Aquinas defines it as a
penalty the sinner imposes on himself. The Homily, however, makes it clear that satisfaction consists not of self-
punishment, but of amendment of life.

> Hereby do we learn what is the satisfaction that God doth require
> of us, which is, that we cease from evil, and do good.
>   p. 544

Posthumus is perfectly aware intellectually of what he needs
to do to be saved. He says:

> Is't enough I am sorry?
> So children temporal fathers do appease;
> Gods are more full of mercy.
>   V, iv, 11–13

This is strongly reminiscent of the language of the Homily:

> For sith that God in the Scriptures will be called our Father,
> doubtless he doth follow the nature and property of gentle and
> merciful fathers . . .
>   p. 526

But although he understands what he must do to repent, he
lacks the faith to do so. He acquires faith when he wit-
nesses a theophany. After his soliloquy he falls asleep, and
Jupiter appears to him in a dream.

In his dream Posthumus's father, mother, and two broth-
ers denounce Jupiter for unjustly punishing their noble
kinsman. Jupiter descends on the back of an eagle, cowing
his accusers by throwing a thunderbolt. He chides the

Leonati for questioning his justice, and explains why he has subjected Posthumus to so much suffering:

> Whom best I love I cross; to make my gift,
> The more delay'd, delighted. Be content;
> Your low-laid son our godhead will uplift.
> His comforts thrive, his trials well are spent.
>
> V, iv, 101–4

As proof that the vision was not merely a dream, Jupiter leaves a book containing a cryptic prophecy of Posthumus's future happiness.

There is a good deal of critical controversy about how we are to understand this scene. The most important question concerns the identity of the deity who appears to Posthumus. He appears in the guise of Jupiter, but is he Jupiter or does he really represent God? Because of the importance of Christian ideas in the play, a number of critics think that Jupiter is really the Christian God. For instance, J. A. Bryant says:

> there is no question of a pagan Jupiter here. Jupiter is the One God, called Jupiter in this play simply because the setting happens to be pre-Christian Britain.[23]

On the other hand, R. G. Hunter, who generally interprets the play in Christian terms, is unwilling to grant that Jupiter is the Christian deity:

> This airborne, sulphurous-breathed old gentleman is not, I think, meant to convey to us the full impact of God's awful majesty.[24]

I think that the truth encompasses both views. Jupiter fills the role of God while retaining his own identity.

---

23. J. A. Bryant, *Hippolyta's View* (Lexington, 1961), p. 200.
24. Hunter, p. 172.

We can be sure that Jupiter fills the role of God because, before he appears to Posthumus, Posthumus is in a state of despair. After he sees Jupiter, Posthumus is filled with new hope and joy:

> Many dream not to find, neither deserve,
> And yet are steep'd in favours; so am I,
> That have this golden chance and know not why.
> V, iv, 130–32

Furthermore, although Posthumus is still ready to meet death fearlessly, his joy at being released from prison shows that he no longer wishes to die.[25] The appearance of Jupiter has given him the faith to complete his repentance. Posthumus now wishes to complete his repentance by amending his life.

However, although Jupiter fills the role of God, he retains his identity as a Roman deity. The lightning-thrower is clearly Jove and not God. Why Shakespeare characterizes him in this way is an interesting question. There was a precedent for showing God on the English stage. Mystery plays—performed in England until late in the sixteenth century—used God as a character. These plays were a product of Catholic times, however, and Shakespeare would, in fact, have been violating a recent law had he tried to introduce God on the stage.[26] There were, furthermore, sound aesthetic reasons not to do so. G. Wilson Knight offers one of the best explanations I have seen.

> We may practically equate Shakespeare's Jove with Jehovah, whilst observing that, since representation of the supreme deity

25. V, iv, 200.
26. The Act of Abuses forbade any person "in any stage play, Interlude, Shewe, Maygame or Pageant jestingly or prophanely [speaking] or [using] the holy Name of God or of Christ Jesus or of the Holy Ghost or of the Trinitie." See E. K. Chambers, *William Shakespeare* (Oxford, 1930), 2: 238.

cannot be completely successful, (as Milton also found) Shakespeare probably gains rather than loses in *Cymbeline* by reliance on a semi-fictional figure allowing a maximum of dignity with a minimum of risk.[27]

Although normally one must be cautious in consulting Mr. Knight as a hierophant, I think he explains this mystery very well.

In the final scene of the play, Iachimo tells Posthumus how he tricked him, and then begs Posthumus to put him to death. Postumus has completed his repentance, however, and has no malice toward his former enemy. He pardons him:

> Kneel not to me.
> The power that I have on you is to spare you,
> The malice towards you, to forgive you. Live
> And deal with others better.[28]
> V, v, 418–21

Posthumus's Christian gesture touches Cymbeline. The King had planned to put the Roman prisoners of war to death, but instead he follows Posthumus's example and pardons them:

> Nobly doom'd!
> We'll learn our freeness of a son-in-law;
> Pardon's the word to all.
> V, v, 421–23

27. *The Crown of Life* (London, 1948), p. 202.

28. Although Iachimo repents, he is not a complex character. Before he repents he is a sterotyped stage villain. After he repents he is left without a character—he is simply faceless. He is like the characters of Ben Jonson's *Everyman Out of his Humor*. Jonson's characters are stereotypes of Elizabethan life who possess one defining trait or "humor," invariably a highly unpleasant one. In the last act each of these characters is humiliated—shamed out of his humor. They acquire no new identities; they simply lose the ones they had.

Posthumus embraces Imogen, and all go off to live happily ever after.

In comparing *Cymbeline* with *Measure for Measure* one finds Posthumus's repentance more convincing dramatically than Angelo's for a number of reasons. For one thing, it is presented in more detail. For another, Posthumus repents before he is caught, and not afterwards, like Angelo. Theologically this makes no difference; it is never too late to repent. God will never despise a contrite heart, the Homily tells us, and nothing brings contrition faster than getting caught. But although the repentances of the two men might be equally valid in the eyes of God, the audience is far more apt to forgive a man who seemingly achieves his pardon, than one who seemingly has it thrust upon him.

Most important, however, *Cymbeline* succeeds, despite its numerous defects, in treating the theme of sin and repentance better than *Measure for Measure* because its form is better adapted for it. The elements of melodrama, serious action and heightened emotions, provide a better medium for a serious theme than complication comedy, with its traditional associations of horseplay and amorality. Furthermore, melodrama is a basically moral form. Traditionally it pits good against evil in an elemental struggle in which good always prevails. Northrop Frye says of it:

> In melodrama two themes are important: the triumph of moral virtue over villainy, and the consequent idealizing of the moral views assumed to be held by the audience.[29]

The moral views of Shakespeare's audience are Christian, and this play deals with specifically Christian concerns: the struggle of chastity against lust, charity against revenge, and repentance against despair. The battle between chastity

---

29. *Anatomy of Criticism* (Princeton, 1957), p. 47.

and lust is fought out in the traditional melodramatic fashion: the chaste heroine is beset by lustful villains. The battles between charity and revenge and repentance and despair are fought out on a different battlefield, the soul of the hero. Thus *Cymbeline* combines the traditional elements of melodrama with a new aspect, the internal, moral struggle of the hero. In this respect it is a transitional play between the crude melodrama of *Pericles* and the sophisticated new form Shakespeare achieves in *The Winter's Tale*, in which he does away completely with black and white characters, and internalizes the whole struggle between good and evil in the soul of the protagonist. Incidentally, he also writes a far better constructed and more effective play.

4

The Winter's Tale:
The Achievement of
an Adequate Form

SHAKESPEARE wrote *The Winter's Tale* directly after *Cymbeline*. Both plays are based on the theme of sin and repentance, and both make strong use of the elements of melodrama. But in *The Winter's Tale* Shakespeare continues the process he began in *Cymbeline*. He further modifies the elements of melodrama to create a dramatic form that allows him to combine a serious theme with a happy ending. Traditionally the struggle between good and evil takes place between stereotyped good and evil characters. But in *The Winter's Tale* the battle is waged within the soul of the protagonist, Leontes. Jealousy and anger finally overpower reason. This moral struggle, in which Leontes first chooses to sin, then to repent, is the essence of the play. Shakespeare depicts Leontes' ordeal in careful detail, far more so than he had that of Posthumus. In fact, Shakespeare treats Leontes' psychological struggle with the same depth as he does those of Macbeth and Othello.

Because of this psychological examination of Leontes, *The Winter's Tale* differs from traditional melodramas. Nevertheless, Shakespeare retains the most important elements of melodrama: sensational, bloody action, strong appeals to the emotions, and a happy ending. In addition, in *The Winter's Tale,* as in *Pericles* and *Cymbeline,* he employs elements of fairy tale or romance.

In *The Winter's Tale,* as in *King Lear,* Shakespeare plunges directly into the problem of moral choice. Only a short expository scene precedes the key situation in which the protagonist succumbs to jealous anger and commits the sinful acts that bring woe to himself, his kin, and his kingdom. When Leontes' friend Polixenes seeks to leave the Sicilian court after a long visit, Leontes tries to persuade him to stay. When Polixenes refuses, Leontes asks his wife Hermione to persuade Polixenes. Hermione succeeds, whereupon suspicion and jealousy overwhelm Leontes. He suspects that the two are lovers. Without waiting to determine guilt or innocence, he orders a courtier, Camillo, to kill Polixenes. Camillo realizes that murder here would also be regicide, and refuses to carry out the order. Camillo justifies his disobedience on the grounds that Leontes is "in rebellion with himself"[1]—that is, his passions have overthrown his reason. It is interesting to note that in Shakespeare's first tragedy of moral choice, *Julius Caesar,* Brutus uses the same image of insurrection to describe his own state of mind.[2]

Camillo warns Polixenes of his danger, and both flee. This act confirms Leontes' suspicions, and he imprisons Hermione. Later, he further humiliates her by subjecting her to public trial on the charge of adultery.

Although jealous wrath drives both Leontes and Posthumus to attempt murder, Leontes is clearly the guiltier of the two. Posthumus is deceived by a clever villain whose Italianate wiles are too subtle for his straightforward

---

1. I, ii, 355.
2. II, i, 68, 69.

victim. Leontes, on the other hand, is not tricked by anyone; he deceives himself. In fact, everyone whom he consults insists that Hermione is innocent. Furthermore, Posthumus has circumstantial evidence against Imogen. Leontes has none. In contrast to Posthumus, Leontes has no excuse for his behavior.

Shakespeare makes a point of deepening Leontes' guilt. Comparing the play with its source, Robert Greene's prose romance *Pandosto* reveals that Shakespeare made a number of changes in the story in order to deprive Leontes of any excuse for his acts. In Greene's tale, Leontes' counterpart, Pandosto, has good reason to suspect his wife, Bellaria, and his friend Egistus. Bellaria intends to show her husband how much she loves him by being especially courteous to Egistus, who is paying a court visit. Unfortunately she overdoes it, and her "honest familiarity," as Greene calls it, increases until there is "such a secret uniting of their affections that the one could not well be without the company of the other."[3] Pandosto becomes aware of their infatuation, and is disturbed by it, as well he might be. However, he acts wrongly in letting his passions control him. Egistus and Bellaria do not consummate their love. They do nothing more sinful than walk in the garden. But Pandosto, inflamed with jealousy, imagines the worst— adultery. He determines to kill Egistus.

Shakespeare deletes from Greene's tale the material that would serve to justify Leontes' jealousy. There is no indication that Hermione, like Bellaria, is infatuated with her husband's friend, or that she acts in any way that would justify Leontes' suspicions. Shakespeare also changes the slow buildup of jealousy in Pandosto to a sudden explosion by Leontes.

---

3. Arden *W. T.*, Appendix IV, p. 186.

It should be made clear that, although Leontes' jealousy is sudden, it is neither unconvincing nor unrealistic. Many critics have argued that the abrupt onset of Leontes' passion renders it suspect, and they treat it as if it were simply one of the unrealistic conventions of romantic drama. Quiller-Couch, editor of the Cambridge edition, says:

> In *Pandosto* (we shall use Shakespeare's names) Leontes' jealousy is made slow and by increase plausible. Shakespeare weakens the plausibility of it as well by ennobling Hermione . . . as by huddling up the jealousy in its motion so densely that it strikes us as merely frantic and—what is worse in drama—a piece of impossible improbability. This has always and rightly offended the critics.[4]

Although this has long been the prevalent view, it seems to me that Leontes' rage is probable enough. Jealousy is by its very nature irrational, and it often makes itself felt suddenly and powerfully. S. L. Bethell explains this very well:

> . . . sinful thoughts such as this unwarranted sexual jealousy, though they may not in reality spring full grown into the mind, may well emerge with baffling suddenness into the consciousness. We are thus shown Leontes' jealousy . . . as it appears to Leontes himself and presumably to those around him.[5]

Robert Hunter agrees, stating that "the soliloquies (more properly asides) in which Leontes presents his diseased psyche to us are among Shakespeare's most brilliant displays of his ability to dramatize the human mind."[6]

These statements are high praise indeed, and, if a bit

---

4. *The Winter's Tale,* ed. Sir Arthur Quiller-Couch and John Dover Wilson (Cambridge, 1931), p. xvi. This edition hereafter referred to as Camb. *W. T.*

5. *The Winter's Tale: A Study* (London, 1947), p. 79.

6. *Shakespeare and the Comedy of Forgiveness* (New York, 1965), p. 186.

too strong, are a needed corrective to the dominant critical opinion that there is little psychological realism in *The Winter's Tale*.

Leontes does not restrict his wrath to his wife and her presumed lover. His mad rage envelops the daughter Hermione bears in prison—Perdita. Convinced that Polixenes is the father, Leontes orders the infant burned alive. His courtiers beg him to soften his decision, and he reluctantly agrees to the slightly less inhumane course of abandoning the child in a "remote and desert place."

Leontes' final sin is blasphemy. To satisfy his courtiers, who believe Hermione to be innocent, he agrees to consult the oracle of Apollo at Delphi, and to abide by its "spiritual counsel." He sends two lords to bring the word from Delphi, and has it read at Hermione's trial. Unlike most oracular statements, this one is perfectly clear:

> Hermione is chaste; Polixenes blameless; Camillo a true subject; Leontes a jealous tyrant; his innocent babe truly begotten; and the King shall live without an heir, if that which is lost is not found.
>
> III, ii, 133–37

The oracle is the voice of Apollo, who here fills the same role as Jupiter does in *Cymbeline:* he represents God. Yet, Leontes dares challenge his word:

> There is not truth at all i' th' Oracle.
> The sessions shall proceed; this is mere falsehood.
> III, ii, 140–41

Apollo punishes this blasphemy instantly. A messenger runs up to tell Leontes that his beloved son, Mamillius, is dead. Leontes realizes immediately why the boy dies. He, Leontes, is being punished:

> Apollo's angry; and the heavens themselves
> Do strike at my injustice.
>
> III, ii, 146–47

Hermione, still in the dock, swoons at the news of her son's death. She is carried off, and her lady-in-waiting, Paulina, returns soon after to report falsely that the Queen is dead.

At this point Leontes repents, but it is too late to recall Antigonus, who has already set out with Perdita. While carrying the infant ashore, Antigonus is attacked and killed by a bear. The manner of his death is a strange one, and I will discuss it at length below. Here I address myself only to the question of Leontes' culpability in Antigonus's death.

At first glance it may seem that Antigonus is an innocent victim of Leontes' madness—that he, like Cordelia, is crushed by the evil forces set loose in the world by a mad and powerful king. To cause the death of an innocent man would be serious enough, but it seems that Leontes' sin is even graver. Leontes is guilty of corrupting an honest man and sending him to his death in a sinful state. Antigonus sins by abandoning Perdita. That he was ordered to do it by his king does not excuse him. (His behavior is in obvious contrast to that of Camillo, who had contrived to evade Leontes' order to kill Polixenes. Later, when Leontes comes to his senses, he realizes that in disobeying the order Camillo was "most humane and filled with honor.") For another thing, it makes no difference that Antigonus swears an oath to carry out the order. Hunter cites the Homily "Of Swearing" on this point:

> If a man at any time shall, either of ignorance or of malice, promise and swear to do anything which is either against the law of Almighty God, or not in his power to perform, let him take it for an unlawful and ungodly oath.[7]

---

7. Hunter, p. 195.

Antigonus receives a supernatural warning that his evil act will cause his death, yet he persists. Hermione appears to him in a dream and tells him that because of the "ungentle business/ Put on thee by my Lord," he will never see his wife again. He is killed the next day. Like Hamlet's father he is cut off in the blossoms of his sin—sent to his account unhouseled, disappointed and unaneled, "with all his imperfections on his head."

In going over the list of Leontes' offenses, we find that he is blacker than the sinners in *Measure for Measure* and *Cymbeline,* Shakespeare's previous repentance plays. Posthumus has some excuse for his sin. Although Angelo has none, he at least struggles manfully against temptation before he succumbs to it. Why does Shakespeare depart from his source to deepen Leontes' guilt? Quite possibly he wants to explore the theme of repentance more fully than he had in earlier plays. In *Measure for Measure* and *Cymbeline* Shakespeare hedges on the repentance theme. The protagonists repent sins they do not commit. Their intended victims escape. Of course, an unsuccessful attempt to commit a forbidden act is sinful, but it is far less serious, especially in its impact on an audience, than the actual commission of the act.

Unlike Posthumus and Angelo, Leontes causes irreparable tragedy—the deaths of Antigonus and Mamillius. Yet he wins redemption. In depicting this redemption, Shakespeare gives a far more meaningful treatment to the theme of sin and repentance than he had in earlier plays. The Homily "Of Repentance" teaches that if a sinner repents, he will be forgiven no matter how serious his sin, no matter what the consequences. Leontes' pardon better illustrates the doctrine of repentance than the pardon of Angelo or Posthumus, who do no worse than cause their intended victims temporary distress and inconvenience.

Leontes begins his repentance when Mamillius dies. He states his intention to follow the Homily's four steps to redemption: contrition, confession, faith, and amendment of life.

> Apollo, pardon
> My great profaneness 'gainst thine oracle!
> I'll reconcile me to Polixenes,
> New woo my queen, recall the good Camillo,
> Whom I proclaim a man of truth, of mercy;
> For, being transported by my jealousies
> To bloody thoughts and to revenge, I chose
> Camillo for the minister to poison
> My friend Polixenes; which had been done,
> But that the good mind of Camillo tardied
> My swift command, though I with death and with
> Reward did threaten and encourage him,
> Not doing't and being done. He, most humane
> And fill'd with honour, to my kingly guest
> Unclasp'd my practice, quite his fortunes here,
> Which you knew great, and to the [certain] hazard
> Of all incertainties himself commended,
> No richer than his honour. How he glisters
> Through my [dark] rust! And how his piety
> Does my deeds make the blacker!
>
> III, ii, 154–73

Leontes' contrition is evident. To use the language of the Homily, he is earnestly sorry for his sins, and laments and bewails that he has offended God. And Leontes fully and openly confesses his sins. He specifically mentions reconciliation with Hermione, Camillo, and Polixenes. The Homily stresses that reconciliation is an important part of confession:

> the faithful ought to acknowledge their offences, whereby some hatred, rancour, ground or malice, having risen or grown among

them one to another that a brotherly reconciliation may be had; without the which nothing that we do can be acceptable unto God.

p. 538

The third and fourth parts of repentance are faith and amendment of life. Leontes clearly states his intention to amend his evil ways. Implicit in his words seems to be the faith that Apollo, Hermione, and his friends will forgive him. Even at his lowest point, when he believes Hermione dead, Leontes does not despair. Rather, out of his mourning for his wife and child he hopes to make a new life:

> Once a day I'll visit
> The chapel where they lie, and tears shed there
> Shall be my recreation.
>
> III, iii, 237–39

"Recreation" means here not only "entertainment," but also spiritual "re-creation."

In one important respect Leontes' repentance follows a different pattern from those of Angelo and Posthumus. He undergoes a protracted period of penance—sixteen years. During that time he disappears from the stage, and the focus of the play shifts to Perdita. The tone shifts also, from one of heavy melodrama to a much lighter one of pastoral complication comedy. The scene in which the bear kills Antigonus and the old shepherd finds Perdita serves as a transition. It links melodrama with comedy by treating a traditional subject of melodrama, bloody death, comically.

For Shakespeare does turn Antigonus's grisly death into comedy. First, we see the bear chase Antigonus, and the chase is a funny one. There has been a good deal of speculation as to how the King's Men staged the scene. Quiller-Couch offers his "private opinion" that "the bear pit in

Southwark, hard by the Globe theatre, had a tame animal to let out, and the management took the opportunity to make a popular hit."[8] J. Dover Wilson cites the contemporary Elizabethan productions *Mucedorus* and *The Masque of Oberon,* which mention white bears, and concludes that "it can hardly be doubted that Antigonus was pursued by a polar bear in full view of the audience of the Globe."[9]

Nevill Coghill, for one, does doubt it. After some zoological research, he concludes that polar bears are far too dangerous to employ in chasing actors. He also doubts that any other kind of bear, even if tame, would be able to perform reliably in the role required. He argues that the bear in *The Winter's Tale* is really a man in a bear suit. This seems to be a reasonable surmise. It seems unlikely that any of the King's Men would be anxious to be chased by a bear on loan from the bear pit where it spent its working hours being tormented for the delight of the paying customers. However, whether the bear is real or not, the scene is comic. Any bear tame enough to be trusted on stage would be funny rather than terrifying, as anyone who has seen a dancing bear can testify. A man waddling around in a bear suit would be even more ludicrous, and would raise a yelp of laughter from the groundlings.

Although Coghill makes more sense than Quiller-Couch or Wilson, some of his ideas, too, are open to question. He argues that the scene is frightening as well as funny because, although the man in the bear suit is comical, "it is terrifying and pitiful to see a bear grapple with an elderly man to a dreadful death. . . ."[10] However, this is

---

8. Camb. *W. T.,* p. xx.
9. *Ibid.,* p. 156.
10. "Six Points of Stagecraft in *The Winter's Tale,*" *Shakespeare Survey,* 11:34.

not what we see. The Folio's stage direction says, "Exit, pursued by a bear." The bear catches and kills Antigonus offstage. We learn what happens from a witness. Since we do not see the action ourselves, our impression of the incident is determined by his account. The witness is a bumbling rustic known only as the Clown. With his description of Antigonus's death the Clown interlards a description of the sinking of Antigonus's ship. Combined, the account is sufficiently disorganized and ludicrous to rob the events of their terror:

> now the ship boring the moon with her main-mast, and anon swallowed with yest and froth, as you'd thrust a cork into a hogshead. And then for the land-service, to see how the bear tore out his shoulder bone, how he cried to me for help and said his name was Antigonus, a nobleman. But to make an end of the ship, to see how the sea flap-dragoned it: but first, how the poor souls roared, and the sea mocked them: and how the poor gentleman roared, and the bear mocked him, both roaring louder than the sea or weather. . . . I have not winked since I saw these sights: the men are not yet cold under water, not the bear half dined on the gentleman; he's at it now.
>
> III, iii, 91–105

Why does Shakespeare make the death of Antigonus comic? For one thing, he wants to soften the audience's attitude toward Leontes. The death of Mamillius and the presumed death of Hermione outrage and shock us, and render Leontes odious. Right after the trial scene it seems doubtful that we will ever be reconciled to seeing Leontes forgiven. But the comic death of Antigonus makes us realize that the play takes place not in a realistic world but in the world of romance, a make-believe world in which death is not necessarily tragic. The comicality of Antigonus's death changes the way we feel about the deaths of

Mamillius and Hermione. The deaths are stripped of their tragic grimness. Perhaps a happy ending will be possible for the man who kills them—if he atones for his sin. In addition, when the shepherd finds Perdita, we realize that this world of romance is a world of second chances. No event, not even death, is final. In this world people come back to life, or are discovered to have been alive all the time.

In short, Antigonus's comic death moves us away from the realistic world of the first part of the play. It prepares us for the happier romantic world of Acts Four and Five, which in turn prepare us for the happy ending in which Hermione is restored to Leontes.

After the death of Antigonus we also move from one phase of the theme, sin, to the other, redemption. When the Clown finishes his description of Antigonus's death, the Shepherd says:

> Now bless thyself; thou met'st with things dying,
> I with things new-born.
>
> III, iii, 117–18

The things dying are the victims of Leontes. The thing new born is Perdita, who brings grace and life to those around her. It is here that the focus of the play shifts from Leontes to Perdita. In the next scene Time, the chorus, describes the shift:

> Leontes leaving,
> The effects of his fond jealousies so grieving
> That he shuts himself up . . .
> To speak of Perdita, now grown in grace
> Equal with wond'ring.
>
> IV, i, 17–25

A number of critics state that "grace" has a theological
as well as physical meaning here—that is, Perdita is not
only graceful but also full of God's grace.[11] Her reunion
with Leontes (as well as his reunion with Hermione) sig-
nals the return of grace to the hero.

Along with the shift in focus upon characters, there is
a shift in setting. We move from the dark court of Leontes'
Sicilia, shrouded with mourning, to the sunny fields of Bo-
hemia. There is also a shift in tone and form. In the first
half of the play, Shakespeare uses heavy melodrama—
bloodshed and violent appeals to the emotions—to show
the destructive effect of sin. Now, to prepare us for Leontes' redemption, he shifts to the lighter tone of comedy.
The action concerning Florizel and Perdita is a play within
a play; it is a complete, if brief, complication comedy,
similar in form to Shakespeare's Elizabethan comedies.
The form derives ultimately from Roman New Comedy.
In fact, the story of Florizel and Perdita is markedly similar to that of Terence's *Andria,* which we looked at in
chapter one. In both, a boy wants to marry a girl of low
social station. When the father's objections seem to doom
the lovers' cause, it turns out that the girl is the long-lost
daughter of the father's best friend.

I am not arguing here that Shakespeare used the *Andria*
as the source for the Florizel-Perdita plot. Obviously
Shakespeare got the main outline of the story from *Pandosto.* What I am arguing is that the story as dramatized
follows the pattern of the typical Roman love comedy: boy
wants to marry girl, but the course of true love never runs
smooth until the final scene. Shakespeare was quite familiar
with this comic form; he uses a variation of it in all his

---

11. See, for instance, Bethell, p. 90, and M. M. Mahood, *Shakespeare's
Wordplay* (London, 1957), p. 152.

Elizabethan comedies. What is significant here is that Shakespeare imbeds a complication comedy within a melodrama. Since he has used both forms separately before, he obviously knows what he is doing, and is aware of the dramatic effect he will create. That effect is, of course, to lighten the tone of the play to prepare the audience for the happy ending for Leontes.

With the opening of Act Five, the focus of the play returns to Leontes. He has undergone his self-imposed penance for sixteen years. It is important to note that in the pattern of repentance and pardon *The Winter's Tale* differs from the earlier repentance plays. In *Measure for Measure* and *Cymbeline,* when the hero repents he is immediately forgiven by those he sins against. More is involved in these pardons, however, than the reconciliation between sinner and victim. The sinner not only asks forgiveness of those he has injured, he repents his sin to God. God's pardon is implicit in the victim's pardon of the sinner.

But when Leontes repents, and states his intention to "new woo his queen," Hermione does not forgive him immediately. Instead, she pretends to be dead and makes Leontes undergo years of mourning and penance. As in other repentance plays, the hero's reconciliation with his loved one symbolizes divine forgiveness. Robert Hunter argues that Hermione functions as "the primary symbol of God's grace and it is her return to Leontes that marks his achievement of forgiveness." Hunter further argues that "the long withdrawal of the visible signs of grace from Leontes is the result of the gods' insistence that he make satisfaction for this sin."[12] If this is true, and it seems to be, it is important to note that Leontes is the first sinner in Shakespeare who must make satisfaction in order to be forgiven.

12. P. 199.

In *Measure for Measure* and *Cymbeline* the heroes do not need to do penance or make satisfaction to be forgiven. Angelo is forgiven as soon as he repents. *Measure for Measure* and *Cymbeline* follow the implications of The Homily "Of Repentance." The Homily plays down the role of penance and satisfaction stressed in the Catholic doctrine that antedates the Homily. The emphasis shifts from making amends to God to amending one's way of life.

Posthumus's mistaken ideas about penance and satisfaction actually delay his redemption by leading him to despair. When he substitutes faith in God for penance and satisfaction, he is forgiven. Leontes, on the other hand, undergoes a period of penance. The language of the play indicates that he does this to make satisfaction to God. Toward the end of Leontes' ordeal Camillo—a purely expository character—says:

> Sir, you have done enough, and have perform'd
> A saint-like sorrow. No fault could you make,
> Which you have not redeem'd; indeed, paid down
> More penitence than done trespass. At the last,
> Do as the heavens have done, forget your evil;
> With them forgive yourself.
>
> > V, i, 1–6

The metaphor is monetary. Leontes' penance is the legal tender with which he pays to God the debt that he incurred with this sin.

Why Shakespeare has Leontes do penance when sinners in earlier plays do not is an interesting question. Perhaps the serious consequences of Leontes' sin have something to do with it.

It is possible, however, that the long penance may be explained by dramatic rather than theological reasons. For one thing, the long period gives Perdita a chance to grow up and fall in love. Her love affair with Florizel is one of the most charming interludes in Shakespeare. It is not unlikely that Shakespeare saw the story in the source, realized its dramatic possibilities, and was loath to leave it out of his play. Another result of the long penance is that audiences are more willing to forgive Leontes than they were the heroes of the earlier repentance plays. Angelo and Posthumus win forgiveness from their victims, and from God, but seldom from the playgoers. The reason is simple. In *Cymbeline,* for instance, Imogen forgives Posthumus because she loves him. God forgives Posthumus because He is infinitely merciful. But the audience has neither Imogen's love nor God's compassion for Posthumus. Playgoers usually feel that Posthumus gets off too lightly. They are even less inclined to forgive Angelo, since he repents after he is exposed.

Leontes is the blackest of the three. Yet we are most willing to forgive him because he suffers the most for his sins. By his protracted penance he wins our pardon. When Hermione forgives him in the statue scene, we are genuinely moved. The denouements of *Measure for Measure* and *Cymbeline* raise no comparable emotions.

At any rate, whatever the reason for the delay, and whatever role penance plays, it is evident that Leontes repents and that God forgives him. In *The Winter's Tale,* as in *Cymbeline,* the hero's restored fortunes indicate God's pardon. This involves, in both plays, a reconciliation with the wife whom the hero thinks he has killed. She is the symbol of God's grace, and when she returns to him, we know that heaven forgives him. Hermione's reunion with Leontes is achieved in a remarkable *coup de théâtre:* Leontes goes to the unveiling of what he believes to be Hermione's statue. As he stands in wonder, Hermione steps down from the pedestal and embraces him.

Shakespeare's ending differs markedly from that of his source. In Greene's tale there is no reconciliation. Bellaria, unlike Hermione, actually dies at her trial. Pandosto mourns her for sixteen years. Then he finds his long-lost daughter and marries her to Egistus's son. However, before Pandosto learns his daughter's identity, he lusts after her himself. When he learns who she is, he broods over his sinfulness. His new feeling of shame intensifies the guilt he already feels for his past sins, and he kills himself.

Shakespeare makes major changes here. Hermione and Leontes live: he to repent, she to forgive him. So, while Greene ends his tale with a "tragicall stratagem," the death of the hero, Shakespeare spares Leontes and changes tragedy to melodrama. And he changes the theme from "the wages of sin is death," to: if a man repent his sin, "the gift of God is eternal life."

A major question about the statue scene needs to be answered: why does Shakespeare resort to such theatrics?

Shakespeare may well have encountered the device in *The Trial of Chivalry,* an anonymous melodrama dating from about 1600. In this play Katherine, a French princess, spurns the love of Frederick of Navarre. When a friend of Frederick's tells her that Frederick has been killed in a duel, Katherine's "flinty heart . . . waxeth tender," and she belatedly realizes that she loves Frederick. The friend takes her to see Frederick's funeral monument, supposedly a life-size statue of white alabaster. When she prays,

> And would to God my prayers might be heard,
> That as the Image of Pigmalion once
> Life might descend into this senceless stone . . .[13]

Frederick steps down and kisses her.

---

13. Student's Facsimile Edition (London, 1912), p. H2.

Although there is no direct evidence that Shakespeare knew *The Trial of Chivalry,* the similarity between the two statue scenes provides strong presumptive evidence that he did. Besides, *The Trial* was performed by the Earl of Derby's Men only a half dozen years or so before Shakespeare wrote *The Winter's Tale,* and we are certain that Shakespeare was in London during that period. It seems probable, then, that in writing a play with strong elements of melodrama, he consciously borrowed from another Elizabethan melodrama.

But showing that Shakespeare found the device ready to expand does not explain why he used it, even though it is a spectacular piece of stagecraft. The answer must be that a realistic scene would be badly out of place here. The whole business of Hermione's disappearance is the stuff of romance, not of real life. It is understandable that a woman might leave a husband like Leontes. But that she would hide herself in the shadow of his castle for years and then emerge is incredible by any standards of realistic behavior. Romance operates, however, according to laws of poetic justice, and according to that standard Hermione's behavior is both understandable and commendable. Leontes deserves to be punished, and Hermione's playing dead is an effective way to do it. Hermione's return therefore calls for an equally romantic device. A realistic reconciliation, with Hermione simply walking up to Leontes and embracing him, would not only be inappropriate, but hopelessly flat dramatically.

Shakespeare takes special pains to show the audience that this is the world of romance. Three times in the final act the characters say of events that they are "like an old tale." In fact, the play is called *The Winter's Tale* because it is like a tale told by an old woman around a winter's fire. Winter's tales thrive on the wondrous, and there is no more suitable ending to Shakespeare's than a statue that comes to life. As Hunter says, "the sense of miracle is overwhelming despite the carefully provided naturalistic explanation."[14]

The statue scene is far more successful than the final scenes of the earlier repentance comedies. Angelo's pardon generally causes resentment, and audiences seldom greet Posthumus's pardon with much enthusiasm. But the reconciliation of Leontes and Hermione is genuinely moving. At a recent production of *The Winter's Tale* at Ashland, Oregon, the statue scene had most of the audience in tears.

I have attempted to show in the foregoing discussion that *The Winter's Tale* continues the modification of the melodramatic form that Shakespeare started in *Cymbeline*. *Pericles*, Shakespeare's first experiment with melodrama, resembles Elizabethan models fairly closely. In *Cymbeline*, Shakespeare makes one important innovation: he introduces a complex protagonist whose moral choice is the mainspring of the play's action. However, in *Cymbeline*, as in *Pericles*, much of the battle between the forces of good and evil takes place between stereotyped characters. But in *The Winter's Tale* Shakespeare places the struggle between good and evil in the soul of the protagonist. The other characters are no longer black and white stereotypes; they are a mixture of good and evil. The only exception is Perdita.

To begin with Hermione: although on one level she symbolizes divine grace, on another she is a very human queen. In a skillful touch, Shakespeare shows her humanness in her testiness at her son, Mamillius, who, she says on one occasion, bothers her past enduring. It is only a

---

14. P. 201.

minor touch to be sure, but it shows that if patience is the mark of a saint, Hermione is merely human.

Paulina, the thorn in Leontes' side, has been assigned a number of allegorical and symbolic roles by the critics. Hunter calls her the personification of Leontes' conscience;[15] Bethell calls her the voice of the Old Covenant;[16] and J. A. Bryant says she stands for Saint Paul.[17] Possibly there is something to these attributions, but it should be pointed out that whether or not Paulina acts as Leontes' conscience, or voices the precepts of Mosaic law, primarily she is a very convincing character with a distinct personality, and in some ways a highly objectionable one at that, which makes believable her functions in the play. She is a persistent nag. The reader feels that there was something appropriate in Antigonus's being killed by a bear, since he had spent his life living with one. Paulina takes obvious pleasure in her histrionics when she tells Leontes that Hermione is dead. She also takes it upon herself to tell him not to repent but to despair of salvation. When she is rebuked by a courtier, she realizes that she has gone too far, and repents her outbreak.

Florizel seems at first glance to be the prototypal Prince Charming of fairy tale, and in many ways he is. However, it is interesting to note that in order to marry Perdita he is willing, like Leontes, to let passion rather than reason be his guide. When Camillo tells him to "be advised" he replies:

> I am: and by my fancy. If my reason
> Will thereto be obedient, I have reason;
> If not, my sense, better pleas'd with madness,
> Do bid it welcome.

                                        IV, iv, 483–85

15. P. 200.
16. P. 88.
17. *Hippolyta's Vision* (Lexington, 1961), p. 216.

Camillo points out, "This is desperate, sir." At first glance it seems that Camillo is right, and that counter to the established pattern in Shakespeare Florizel is able to subordinate his reason to his emotions, defy authority, and yet emerge not only unscathed but with Perdita and happiness. However, there are circumstances involved that may explain the apparent contradiction. In the first place, the issue at stake—whether Florizel is to obey his father and marry someone of suitable social station, or whether he should marry Perdita as he has promised her—is not a real issue. Since Perdita is really a princess he can have it both ways. Instinctively, since blood will tell—and always does in fairy tales and romances (witness Cinderella, or for that matter, Orlando in *As You Like It*)—he realizes this, and his fancy and reason are not really in opposition.

Furthermore, it should be noted that, if there was one situation in which the Elizabethans sympathized with following one's emotions and defying authority, it was the case of lovers whose parents objected to their marriage. Or so the dramatists lead us to suppose—witness Juliet or Desdemona or Imogen.

Camillo is primarily the prototype of the good and faithful servant, but he is not above manipulating Florizel and Perdita for his own selfish ends.

Autolycus is one of the most striking of Shakespeare's characters. Although Shakespeare's genius stamps Autolycus with a unique identity, he is derived in part from traditional models. In classical mythology Autolycus was the prototypal thief. Ovid describes him (in Golding's translation) as "a wyly pye / And such a fellow as in theft and filching had no peere."[18] The description, though brief, suggests just the sort of confidence man that Shakespeare creates. Another possible model for Shakespeare's Autoly-

18. XI, 359–63.

cus is the Vice of the morality play, a primarily comic figure devoted to wrongdoing. In particular, Autolycus resembles the Vices in the early romantic dramas—Common Conditions in the play of the same name, and Subtle Shift in the melodrama *Clyomon and Clamydes*. Although the Vice in the morality plays is almost always punished in the denouement, Common Conditions and Subtle Shift escape censure. So, of course, does Autolycus.

The only stereotyped character in the play is Perdita, a typical fairy-tale princess. Although she is charming— the prettiest low-born lass to run across the greensward— she is faceless, merely a paler version of Imogen. She has the same charm but much less spunk.

Since *The Winter's Tale* has no villains, the ending is different from that of traditional melodrama, in which the good characters live happily ever after while the evil characters die violent deaths. Here the characters who die, Antigonus and Mamillius, are sympathetic. Antigonus, as we have noted, is not innocent, but he is certainly not a villain. Mamillius is completely innocent. His death makes Leontes realize for the first time that he has acted sinfully. In a sense this resembles a melodramatic motif common today. In many cowboy movies and war films the hero, like Achilles, sulks in his tent until a traumatic event arouses him—his best friend is killed. Then he sallies forth against the enemy. In the war between good and evil that takes place in Leontes' soul, the forces of good lie dormant until awakened by the death of Mamillius.

So, despite the modifications in the melodramatic form, *The Winter's Tale* retains most of the characteristics of melodrama: the sensational action and bloody deaths, the battle between good and evil, the violent appeals to the emotions, and the happy ending. By combining these elements with psychological realism, complication comedy, and romance, Shakespeare achieves a dramatic form that is excellently suited to convey the theme of repentance. With this form Shakespeare is able to make Leontes' repentance convincing and acceptable to the audience to a greater degree than he had with Angelo and Posthumus.

5
The Tempest: An Epilogue

CRITICS traditionally have grouped *The Tempest,* Shakespeare's final play, with its immediate predecessors—*Pericles, Cymbeline,* and *The Winter's Tale.* True enough, *The Tempest* has some things in common with the other three late plays. It employs elements of romance— fantasy, pastoral setting, idealized love. It also deals with the theme of sin and repentance. Nevertheless, it belongs to a different genre from the preceding plays. *Pericles, Cymbeline,* and *The Winter's Tale* are variations of melodrama. *The Tempest* is a comedy. There is an important difference, too, in the way the theme of sin and repentance is employed in *The Tempest.* The focus of the earlier plays is on the sinners, and while Prospero undoubtedly sinned in neglecting his duties as Duke of Milan, the action of *The Tempest* focuses on him in the aspect of one sinned *against.* Like Posthumus and Leontes of the earlier plays, Prospero is faced with a moral choice. But his choice is not whether to sin or not to sin; it is whether to forgive those who have sinned against him. As for form, melodrama, as we have already seen, employs sensational bloody action. The villains die bloody deaths. In comedy, bloodshed is rare and villains are pardoned rather than slaughtered. Moreover, while melodrama stirs violent emotions in the audience, comedy evokes a much milder response.

By these yardsticks, *The Tempest* is clearly a comedy. Unlike *Pericles, Cymbeline* and *The Winter's Tale, The Tempest* is free of bloodshed. Moreover, the tone is lighter. The forces of good completely dominate the forces of evil. Prospero battles evil characters—Sebastian and Antonio. But, in contrast to the earlier romances—in which villains are strong enough to oppress the sympathetic characters— in *The Tempest* Prospero is so powerful that he toys with his enemies. In tone and ending, *The Tempest* is closer to *The Merchant of Venice, Much Ado about Nothing* and *As You Like It* than it is to the plays that preceded it. In its serious treatment of repentance, however, it is similar to *Cymbeline* and *The Winter's Tale*.

Prospero's power comes from theurgy—white magic. The theurgist achieves his power through learning and virtue. Frank Kermode describes Prospero's art as "the disciplined exercise of virtuous knowledge," or as R. H. West puts it, "a translation of merit into power."[1] This art enables Prospero to command spirits. Chief of his supernatural helpers is Ariel, an invisible and immortal being who combines the characteristic Neo-Platonic daemon and English fairy.[2] Among Ariel's powers are the ability to transport himself from one place to another instantaneously, to know instantly everything that happens, and to be able to control the elements.

The evil characters, lacking special powers, are no match for Prospero and Ariel. The crime they attempt is rebellion, a familiar theme in Shakespeare. It is a major concern of *Julius Caesar* and *Macbeth* as well as most of the history plays. Shakespeare considers rebellion a heinous sin. His ideas have been shown to come in large part from two

---

1. Arden *Tempest* (London, 1954), p. xlvii.
2. *Ibid.*, p. 142.

Homilies, "An exhortation concerning Good Order and Obedience To Rulers and Magistrates," and "Against Disobedience and Wilful Rebellion."[3] "Against Wilful Rebellion" calls rebellion worse than murder:

> For he that nameth rebellion, nameth not a singular or one only sin, as is theft, robbery, murder, and such like; but he nameth the whole puddle and sink of all sins against God and man. . . .[4]

Three rebellions play a part in *The Tempest*. The first, which took place twelve years before the play opens, is described to us by Prospero. In it Antonio supplants Prospero as Duke of Milan. The other two rebellions take place during the course of the play: Sebastian tries to assassinate Antonio in order to seize the throne of Naples, and Caliban tries to wrest control of the island from Prospero.

Prospero lost his kingdom because he was totally immersed in his studies, leaving the ruling of Milan to his brother, Antonio. Not satisfied to rule in Prospero's name, Antonio enlisted the aid of Alonso, King of Naples, to depose the oblivious Prospero. In return for helping Antonio, Alonso demanded that Milan pay tribute and do homage to Naples. Antonio has not only rebelled against his lawful sovereign, Prospero, but betrayed his city as well. The usurpers also attempted to take Prospero's life. The carefully controlled shipwreck at the beginning of *The Tempest* sets the tone for the play. What appears at first to be a disaster turns out to be an exercise in magic by Prospero and Ariel. Here and throughout the play, Prospero and Ariel exert through their magic a benevolent control over the action. Nothing happens without their knowledge and permission. Sebastian's rebellion against Alonso takes place, in a sense, under their supervision. It

---

3. Hart, *Homilies,* p. 70.
4. *Ibid.,* p. 507.

is part of a test Prospero conducts to see if Antonio is still as evil as he was twelve years ago. As Alonso, Sebastian, Antonio, and some courtiers are sitting lamenting their predicament on the island, Ariel charms everyone to sleep but Sebastian and Antonio. Prospero's brother, Antonio, shows that he has not changed. He urges Sebastian to kill Alonso and take over the Neapolitan throne. When Antonio and Sebastian draw their swords, Ariel awakens Alonso and the other courtiers, and the rebellion fails.

The third rebellion is a parody of the other two. Caliban, Prospero's "servant monster," leads Stephano, a butler, and Trinculo, a jester, in an attempt to kill Prospero. Caliban resents Prospero because he, Caliban, was a native of the island and his "own king" before Prospero came and made a slave of him. Distasteful as colonialism and slavery may be to us today, Shakespeare clearly felt that as a civilized European Prospero had a right—indeed, an obligation—to rule a "salvage" like Caliban. And in the case of Prospero and Caliban there is also a moral question. Not only does Prospero represent education and civilization as opposed to Caliban's ignorance and savagery, Prospero represents good and Caliban evil. Prospero's theurgy is holy magic. It allows him to free himself from the world of the flesh. Frank Kermode argues that, in a sense, Prospero's art becomes a means of grace.[5]

Caliban is the son of a witch and a devil. His mother, Sycorax, practiced goety or black magic, and hence her power came chiefly from her ability to command devils.

Prospero was a benevolent colonialist at first, educating Caliban, and learning in return the secrets of the island. It was when Caliban attempted to ravish Miranda that Prospero punished him by making him a slave.

Describing Caliban as the son of a devil and witch may

---

5. Arden *Tempest,* p. 1.

give the impression that he is a formidable creature. He is not. He is primarily a comic figure. He inherits his mother's ugliness and ill will but few of her powers. In mistaking a drunken butler for a god, Caliban shows none of the cunning we would expect of a devil. Prospero does not take Caliban's revolt seriously. Ariel toys with the drunken trio, leading them deep into a stagnant pond, and then routing them with spirits disguised as hounds.

The punishment of Antonio, Alonso, and Sebastian is equally severe, if somewhat less degrading. Ariel appears to them in the form of a harpy and accuses them of deposing Prospero. Ariel tells them that as a result of this sin they shall suffer "ling'ring perdition . . . in this most desolate isle." He tells Alonso that his son, Ferdinand, who has been separated from the others in the wreck, has died because of Alonso's sin. Alonso is in despair. Antonio and Sebastian are defiant. Ariel charms all three into fits of madness.

In the denouement Prospero restores their senses and confronts them. Alonso repents immediately:

> Thy dukedom I resign and do entreat
> Thou pardon me my wrongs.
> > V, i, 118–19

Antonio remains defiant, but Prospero forgives him anyway:

> For you, most wicked sir, whom to call brother
> Would even infect my mouth, I do forgive
> Thy rankest fault—all of them . . .
> > V, i, 130–33

Antonio refuses to repent even then; he does not answer. Sebastian likewise remains mute and defiant. The savage

Caliban proves that he is less barbaric than the sophisticated Antonio and Sebastian when he repents:

> Pro: As you look
>   To have my pardon, trim it handsomely.
>
> Cal: Ay, that I will, and I'll be wise hereafter
>   And seek for grace.
>   V, i, 292–95

Grace here means not only Prospero's favor, but God's
grace.

Faced with the choice of revenge or forgiveness, Prospero decides to pardon his enemies—whether they repent
or not. This choice provides the climax of the play. Ariel,
the inhuman spirit, reminds Prospero that mercy is the
proper human response:

> Ari: . . . Your charm so strongly works 'em
>   That if you now beheld them, your affections
>   Would become tender.
>
> Pro: Dost thou think so, spirit?
>
> Ari: Mine would, sir, were I human.
>   V, i, 17–19

Prospero shows his humanity:

>   And mine shall.
>   Hast thou, which art but air, a touch, a feeling
>   Of their afflictions, and shall not myself,
>   One of their kind, that relish all as sharply
>   Passion as they, be kindlier mov'd than thou art?
>   V, i, 20–24

Prospero makes the correct moral choice because he
allows reason rather than anger to dictate his course:

> Though with their high wrongs I am struck to th' quick,
> Yet with my nobler reason 'gainst my fury
> Do I take part. The rarer action is
> In virtue than in vengeance.
>
> V, i, 25–28

It is important to note the contrast between Prospero and Posthumus and Leontes. Posthumus and Leontes sinfully sought vengeance because they let their fury overrule their reason. It is also important to note the difference in focus. In *Cymbeline* and *The Winter's Tale* the focus is on the sinners, Posthumus and Leontes. In *The Tempest* the focus is on the victim, Prospero. Prospero is a man more sinned against than sinning. His moral choice is whether to revenge or pardon. He pardons.

In summary, in his last play, *The Tempest*, Shakespeare continues his examination of the theme of sin and repentance. But there are no spectacular deaths in *The Tempest*, as there are in *Pericles, Cymbeline*, and *The Winter's Tale*. In *The Tempest*, as in *The Merchant of Venice* and *Much Ado about Nothing*, evil characters threaten harm, but blood is never shed. In *The Tempest*, therefore, Shakespeare abandons the bloody world of melodrama and returns to the sunnier world of romantic comedy.

The Tempest, which shifted its focus from the sinner to the sinned against, completed Shakespeare's experiments in the dramatic use of repentance. As we have seen, Shakespeare returned to the theme of repentance throughout his career. He first used it in *Two Gentlemen of Verona, Much Ado about Nothing*, and *All's Well That Ends Well*.

In these complication comedies Shakespeare did not attempt to make a serious psychological examination of characters who sin and repent. Rather, he used sin and repentance to create and resolve the plays' central complication. In writing his tragedies, however, Shakespeare became deeply interested in the effects of sin on the psyche of his heroes. With his Christian background, it was only natural that he should want to show the redemption of a sinful hero. But this required the happy ending that is unavailable in tragedy.

So, in search of a vehicle for a serious treatment of his theme of sin and redemption, Shakespeare tried comedy. But when, in *Measure for Measure,* he attempts to examine seriously his protagonist's sin and repentance, the contrived conventions of complication comedy compromised the effective statement of the theme. Still searching, Shakespeare therefore turned in *Cymbeline* to a variation of what today we call melodrama. It combined serious tone and action with a happy ending, and so was better able to handle a serious theme than complication comedy. To make melodrama work for his theme, Shakespeare modified the form by adding to the typical stereotyped characters a psychologically complex protagonist. Then, in *The Winter's Tale,* Shakespeare discarded stereotypes altogether and internalized the struggle between the forces of good and evil within the soul of the protagonist. In this play Shakespeare achieved his most successful treatment of the theme of sin and repentance, for the protagonist's repentance was both convincing and emotionally acceptable to the audience.

Shakespeare's experimentation did not end there, for he went on to examine the sin-repentance theme from the point of view of the one sinned *against.* Here he reverted to comedy. In *The Tempest* Prospero's moral choice is not whether to repent his sins, but whether to forgive those who have sinned against him.

By following Shakespeare's treatment of repentance from *Two Gentlemen* to *The Tempest,* we can learn a good deal about the relationship of form and theme. To fully explore a theme that interested him, Shakespeare experimented with different forms until he finally hit upon one that successfully enabled him to accomplish his goal—the probing psychological exploration of men who sin, repent, and achieve redemption.

Bibliography

Baldwin, Thomas W. *William Shakespeare's Five Act Structure.* Urbana, Ill., 1947.

———. *William Shakespeare's Small Latine & Lesse Greeke.* 2 vols. Urbana, 1944.

Bethell, Samuel L. *The Winter's Tale: A Study.* London, 1947.

Bloomfield, Morton. *The Seven Deadly Sins.* East Lansing, Mich., 1952.

Bradley, Andrew C. *Shakespearean Tragedy.* 23d ed. New York, 1955.

Bryant, J. A. *Hippolyta's View.* Lexington, 1961.

Bullough, Geoffrey. *Narrative and Dramatic Sources of Shakespeare.* 4 vols. New York, 1957–1961.

Certain Sermons or Homilies Appointed to be Read in Churches in the Time of Queen Elizabeth of Famous Memory. Oxford, 1844.

Chambers, Edmund K. *Shakespeare: A Survey.* London, 1925.

———. *William Shakespeare, A Study of Facts and Problems.* 2 vols. Oxford, 1930.

Coghill, Nevill. "Six Points of Stagecraft in *The Winter's Tale.*" *Shakespeare Survey* 11 (1958): 31–41.

Dowden, Edward. *Shakespere.* New York, 1878.

Duckworth, George. *The Complete Roman Drama.* 2 vols. New York, 1942.

Farmer, John S. *Five Anonymous Plays.* London, 1908.

———. *Lost Tudor Plays.* London, 1907.

Frye, Northrop. *Anatomy of Criticism.* Princeton, 1957.

Frye, R. M. *Shakespeare and Christian Doctrine.* Princeton, 1963.

Greene, Robert. *The Works of Robert Greene*. Edited by Alexander Grosart. 15 vols. London, 1881–1886.

Harbage, Alfred. *Annals of English Drama 975–1700*. Revised by S. Schoenbaum. London, 1964.

Hunter, Robert G. *Shakespeare and the Comedy of Forgiveness*. New York, 1965.

Knight, G. Wilson. *The Crown of Life*. London, 1948.

Lascelles, Mary. *Shakespeare's Measure for Measure*. London, 1953.

Lawrence, William W. *Shakespeare's Problem Comedies*. New York, 1931.

Muir, Kenneth. *The Last Periods of Shakespeare, Racine and Ibsen*. Detroit, 1961.

Peele, George. *The Works of George Peele*. Edited by A. H. Bullen. 2 vols. London, 1888.

Pettet, E. C. *Shakespeare and the Romantic Tradition*. London, 1949.

Rose, H. J. *A Handbook of Latin Literature*. New York, 1960.

Strachey, J. St. Loe. *Beaumont and Fletcher*. 2 vols. New York, 1949.

Tillyard, E. M. W. *Shakespeare's Last Plays*. London, 1962.

———. *Shakespeare's Problem Plays*. London, 1951.

Wells, Stanley. "Shakespeare and Romance." *Later Shakespeare*. Stratford-Upon-Avon Studies 8 (London, 1966) : 49–61.

Wenzel, Siegfried. *The Sin of Sloth*. Chapel Hill, 1967.

Whitaker, Virgil K. "Philosophy and Romance in Shakespeare's 'Problem' Comedies." *The Seventeenth Century: Studies in the History of English Thought and Literature from Bacon to Pope*. Stanford, 1951.

———. *Shakespeare's Use of Learning*. San Marino, 1964.

Index

125

The Library
Lynchburg College
Lynchburg, Virginia 24504